AN UNSHAKABLE MIND

DISCARD

AN
UNSHAKABLE
MIND

How to Overcome Life's Difficulties

Ryuho Okawa

Lantern Books • New York
A Division of Booklight Inc.

Lantern Books
A Division of Booklight Inc.
One Union Square West, Suite 2001
New York, NY 10003

Library of Congress Cataloging-in-Publication Data

Okawa, Ryuho, 1956–
[Fudoshin. English]
An unshakable mind : how to overcome life's difficulties /
Ryuho Okawa.
p. cm.
Translation of: Fudoshin.
ISBN 1-930051-77-8 (alk.)
1. Spiritual life—Buddhism. 2. Maturation (Psychology)
—Religious aspects. 3. Self-confidence—Religious aspects—
Buddhism. I. Title.
BQ5612 .O53 2002
291.4'4—dc21
2002152401

TABLE OF CONTENTS

PREFACE

The purpose of this book, *An Unshakable Mind*, is to explain how to achieve spiritual growth, based on an understanding of the spirit world.

An unshakable mind cannot be acquired overnight. First it is necessary to construct a solid base, like that of an iceberg, which remains hidden underwater. This is the reason I have devoted a whole chapter to explaining what I call "The Principle of Accumulation," the second chapter of this work.

In Chapter Three, "Confronting Anxiety and Distress," I talk about the manifestations of an unshakable mind, while Chapter Four, "Spiritual Influences As the Cause of Suffering," and Chapter Five, "Overcoming Negative Influences" analyze the background to suffering and suggest concrete ways of overcoming it.

I hope and pray that this book will provide a light in the darkness, to guide those who are exploring and living in accordance with the Truth.

Ryuho Okawa
President
The Institute for Research in Human Happiness
June 1997

CHAPTER ONE

The Iceberg of Life

1. The Foundations for Life

In this book I would like to discuss the subject of how to overcome life's difficulties and suffering from a variety of angles. The central theme is an unshakable mind. I would like to begin by considering the foundations upon which to build a life. In everything, whether or not firm foundations have been established is of vital importance. This is as true for an individual as it is for a large corporation; without a firm base, an individual or a company will be weak. The same can be said about any type of work. In every aspect of life, strong foundations are important.

It can be said that the main purpose of a school education is to construct strong foundations upon which people build their lives. Those who have negative views of education systems often criticize education in schools as a waste of time, saying that individuals should be free to study whatever they like and however much they want.

However, it cannot be denied that a well-rounded education is beneficial in creating firm foundations for life.

During the course of our lives we have to make decisions and take action on many different issues. We need
information and reasons upon which to base those decisions and actions. Without a store of knowledge, this is
impossible. Cooking is a good example of this. If you have
the necessary foundations you can make different dishes
every day. To be able to prepare meals continuously, you
need to have a basic knowledge of cooking and know
dozens, or even hundreds of recipes which constitute the
basis of your culinary skills.

Another example is driving. To drive, you have to
know the traffic rules and regulations, and how to cope
with a variety of situations such as driving on slopes,
driving in rain, at night and passing oncoming cars in
narrow streets. This knowledge provides you with the
necessary information to make decisions. However, if you
are ignorant of the rules, you will not know what to do
when you meet an oncoming car, or how to make a right
or left turn. Only with a knowledge of traffic rules and
regulations can you drive in the correct manner.

In the same way, it is very important to have firm
foundations in life. The more solid and comprehensive
these foundations, the more profound your decisions and
actions will be. You should sometimes look at yourself
and ask if you are making a daily effort to strengthen the
foundations upon which you base your life. If these foun-

dations are inadequate, you will find that in many situations things do not go smoothly.

Foundation building should not just be limited to childhood. Even as an adult, you should continue to build tirelessly. A tree grows bigger and bigger because it never ceases to absorb water and nourishment up through its roots. Even after it has grown tall, it still needs to continue drawing up water and nourishment, otherwise it would die within a week. Trees that live for hundreds of years continue tirelessly to draw water and nourishment up through their roots all their life.

This applies to human beings too. You cannot say that since you are already a full-grown "tree," you do not need water or nourishment; actually it is important that you continue to absorb what you need on a daily basis, in order to strengthen your foundations. Human beings have a tendency to place importance on producing, but if they focus only on producing without taking in the new, before long they will become exhausted.

The same can be said for professions. For instance, there is a world of difference between a pharmacist who continues to acquire and absorb new information about drugs and one whose knowledge has not increased since graduating from university. This is also true of company employees. There can be no comparison between those who simply do the work they are given and those who constantly study, acquiring new information about economics or other knowledge useful for doing a better job.

This difference is especially apparent among engineers. Those who are always experimenting day after day, looking to improve their skills, will eventually succeed in developing new forms of technology in the future. The same applies to doctors; if a doctor continues to study many different fields and is able to understand people's suffering, he or she will be recognized as a good doctor.

So rather than being satisfied with foundations established once and then neglected, it is important that you strive on a daily basis to strengthen the foundations upon which you base your life. Even if they may not be of immediate use to you, you need to build foundations that will stand you in good stead in three, five or even ten years down the road.

2. The Shape of an Iceberg

The foundations upon which we base our lives can be compared to the shape of an iceberg that drifts across the ocean. The part of the iceberg that can be seen above the water only accounts for ten or twenty percent of the total; beneath lies the larger block of ice. Although the part that is visible may look very small, the part that is underwater is surprisingly large.

An iceberg needs to have a large base so as to be stable as it floats on the water. I believe that we should study it and emulate its shape. What can we learn from this shape? The answer is stability. Instead of the whole form of the iceberg being exposed above the surface of the ocean, a large section of it always remains beneath the water. The iceberg displaces water which then generates an upward buoyant force and keeps the iceberg afloat.

Similarly in life, as the part beneath the surface becomes bigger, the buoyancy will also become greater. The part that cannot be seen above the surface corresponds to the part of you that is not seen by others. Every single person has a surface self that others see and an inner self that is not visible to other people. Usually those whose inner self is far larger than the surface self are considered to possess greatness of character. It is unlikely that you regard someone you can see straight through as worthy of admiration. A truly great person has profound inner depths and radiates a subtle, refined light.

In short, greatness of character is dependent on the extent of a person's foundations, the part that remains hidden. Those who reveal only a fraction of themselves and have a vast amount hidden underneath maintain their stability. So when you are working to create the foundations upon which to build your life, it is important that you remember to model yourself on the iceberg.

3. Withstanding Life's Storms

One of the outstanding characteristics of an iceberg is its stability in the face of storms. Even though an iceberg floats on the sea, it remains as stable as terra firma. It resembles an aircraft carrier in that you can walk on it without feeling any movement. Surely this is the secret to withstanding the storms of life. Those who have built solid foundations as a base for their lives will be able to withstand any criticism or censure, and overcome suffering or setbacks.

It is often said that when people are young they should read as many novels as possible. The reason is that through reading novels you can learn lessons about life that lie outside your own personal experience. You cannot change the environment in which you were born and raised and there is a limit to the number of people you can meet in the course of your life. In most cases, people experience the joys, sadness and pain among just a small group of people. Through novels, however, you can learn about the lives of people who live in totally different environments and, by identifying with a main character, you are able to learn more deeply about life.

In this way, novels can enrich your store of wisdom about life. Seeing the characters face and overcome various difficulties, you can identify with them and become determined to face your own problems in just the same way. Of all the many sufferings in life, there are very few that have not been used as the theme of a novel. The most common problems that individuals confront and suffer from are finding a job, marriage and illness; most of these have been used at some time as themes of novels by great writers.

If you read these books, you can solve your problems with the help of those who have a higher perspective. The causes of your distress and difficulties will appear quite obvious to a person with a more profound understanding of human life. A single book can provide you with clues to help you solve your problems and in this way you can reduce your suffering.

You can learn not only from novels but also from history books. Of course no one has ever lived exactly the same life as you, and although another's situation might not be identical, there must be many others who have found themselves with difficulties similar to those you now face. By coming to know how those people managed to overcome the difficulties they faced, you will be able to learn methods for solving problems in life.

As well as novels and history books, there is another kind of writing that brings comfort to people in times of suffering or sadness—the works of great poets. When you encounter a poem that moves you, you may experience great peace as you realize someone else is describing your present situation, and expressing the same feelings that you have. Great poets have penetrating eyes that see through life; their poems can melt the hearts of readers.

The same is true of great art. A beautiful picture can bring much comfort. A single beautiful painting on the wall of a café enriches your soul. Art can sometimes heal the wounds people carry in their hearts. The same is true of fine music, too. When you listen to a masterpiece, the vibrations of your soul become attuned to the refined vibrations of the composer and the music transports you to a world of great peace.

You can also use religion to solve your problems. If you cannot find a solution in novels, history books or art, you may find guideposts for life in the words of great saints or religious leaders of the past. From ancient times, Shakyamuni Buddha, Jesus Christ and Confucius were great teachers because they were able to see through problems in life and provide prescriptions for solving them, using their superior intellects. So when worries are going round and round in your head, you can dissolve them by reading and studying the philosophies of these great teachers.

This is one of the objectives of this book. I am writing it so that people whose minds are constantly agitated, who suffer with worries, or who are always experiencing ups and downs may be able to find salvation. If even a single line of my writings brings you peace and serves as a support for you, I will be satisfied.

To sum up what I have been saying here, learning from the wisdom of great figures and artists will enlarge the foundations that lie beneath the surface, which in turn will help you to withstand the storms of life. So, try to accumulate more wisdom so that you can stand against any difficulty. You need to have strong foundations that will not be affected by the wind, no matter how fiercely it blows across the surface of the ocean.

4. A Sense of Great Stability

From the natural wonder of an iceberg, we need to learn a sense of great stability. Most of the sorrow and suffering experienced during the course of a life has its origin in a lack of stability. Of those you have met, whom do you most admire? What kind of people did you respect and consider great? Did you ever think that anyone whose mind was unsteady and whose moods swung constantly from anger to sadness to happiness all in a single day was worthy of admiration? You probably did not want to be like that.

Those you look up to as embodying your ideals are the kind of people that you want to emulate. These people have a common trait—there is a sense of stability about the way they live. This is one of the secrets of becoming a leader. The quality required of a leader is a sense of stability. It is not the stability of a train that simply runs along the rails, but a stability that stands strong amid problems, no matter what kind of troubles you are confronted with.

As I have already explained, one of the factors that creates this sense of stability is the accumulation of wisdom. Those who possess this stability have a store of wisdom; they know when and what kind of problems people in the past faced and how these people solved them, and they can apply the same methods to solve their own difficulties. When solving difficulties, it is important to be able to see situations from a higher perspective.

If your emotions are unstable, changing from day to day, it is because you are wrestling with a problem and you are in a deadlock, unable to see who is winning, you or the problem. Until the match is over you have no way of knowing if you are the winner or the loser and, as a result, your mind wavers. Take sumo wrestling as an example. Is there any possibility that you could win a sumo match against a grand champion? In almost every case, an ordinary person would have absolutely no chance at all against a professional sumo wrestler; he would be pushed out of the ring and lose the match in an instant. The gap in skills is simply too great.

Professional sumo wrestlers practice in the ring every day so they become strong, developing powerful muscles, solidity and speed. When faced with someone like this, the ordinary person would have no hope of defeating the professional; he would not be able to exert enough strength and naturally would be defeated, even more quickly than he expected.

The same can be said of encountering troubles in life. If you do not have much confidence in yourself, the people you have problems with will seem stronger and more difficult to deal with than they actually are, and problems will appear very serious. As a result, you will go weak at the knees, as if you were facing a great sumo wrestler. However, if you became a great champion yourself, you would find that your problems could be solved with surprising ease.

So before you start to worry about how to solve your problems, develop the strength of a grand champion so that any problems will seem like minor matters that can easily be solved. A professional sumo wrestler can carry in one hand a load that is too heavy for the ordinary person to carry even a few paces on his back.

If people train themselves, they will develop in stature. When it comes to physical training, there is a limit to how much you can increase your abilities. In the case of the hundred meter sprint, a fast runner may be able to finish in a little under ten seconds, but even a slow runner will be able to finish in under twenty seconds. So with regard to physical strength, the differences between the abilities of best and worst would be double at the most. However, in the case of inner strength, a huge difference exists between the exceptional person and the ordinary one. For example, there is a huge difference between the intelligence of Socrates and that of the ordinary person, just as there is a huge difference in the wisdom of Shakyamuni Buddha and that of an ordinary priest.

The more the inner self is trained, the greater the ability and the brilliance that develop; there are no limits to the extent of this increase. There are limits to the degree to which physical strength can be developed, but inner strength can be developed a thousand fold or ten thousand fold. If you were to become a spiritual giant, the problems you now regard as matters of life and death would seem very easy to solve.

When you find yourself faced with a huge problem, another important key is to try to imagine how some great person would approach it. For instance, if you are Christian, you may ask yourself what Jesus Christ would think of your problem and how he would go about solving it. Suppose you are suffering because you find it impossible to forgive someone, and you mull over your resentment until you are unable to sleep at night. If this happens, you should try to change your perspective and imagine what Jesus Christ would do or what advice he would give you.

If you are Buddhist, you might ask yourself what Shakyamuni Buddha would say about your problem and how he would solve it. Or you could imagine what Confucius would do in your position, or Socrates. This is a very useful method to adopt when viewing problems. When judging situations and coping with difficulties, it is helpful to try to borrow from the wisdom of great figures.

To create a strong sense of stability, it is necessary to achieve a higher level of inner strength and accumulate spiritual wisdom. Here lies the source of stability. If you wish to become a spiritual giant, it is not enough just to face and grapple with the problems you encounter in the course of your life; it is also essential that you learn lessons from each of them.

The lessons that you learn in this way will stand you in good stead later. A problem that you had difficulty solving the first time will be easy to settle the next time you encounter it because you have managed to overcome it before. For this reason, you should not spend your time aimlessly but make an effort to learn the lesson from each of the incidents and problems that you face daily. These lessons are what you need to learn in life, and they form the foundations of a wisdom that is rarely taught in schools.

How many drawers of lessons have you accumulated? The quantity and quality of the lessons in those drawers are closely related to your degree of awareness and your decision-making ability. From this point of view, it can be said that those who have undergone many experiences, who have known constant hardship and experienced many failures, setbacks and problems, will have had the opportunity to learn a lot of lessons. They have not just spent their days aimlessly; they have been given a workbook with a series of problems to be solved, so it can be said they have been blessed.

When you are faced with a problem and you find yourself in a whirlpool of suffering, you should not simply try to get out of it. Instead, find out what this problem is trying to teach you and what kind of lessons it is providing you with. This will lead you to solve it. Everything has a meaning and it is your job to find out what it is.

5. Sustaining Will

I would like to finish this chapter by talking about the importance of sustaining will. In the previous section, I explained what constitutes the foundations of stability, but the effort to attain this stability should not just be temporary. If you consistently aim to progress on a daily basis, this in itself produces a great sense of stability.

Take an Antarctic icebreaker, for example. As long as it keeps on moving forward, it will smash its way through the ice. However, once it stops, the ice will build up and it will become trapped. The same is true in life; to avoid being trapped, you have to keep on moving forward. Grow daily through your experiences, and always keep in mind that with each new lesson you learn you become spiritually stronger and healthier.

Your stability should not hold for just one situation or at one time. You need the kind of stability that will lead you to find solutions for any problem you may have to face. To that end, it is important to have the determination to progress and to improve yourself constantly. For those who always aspire to develop, to improve and advance, life's worries will simply be resolved with time, like the dew in the morning that evaporates as the sun rises.

First, make the sun within you rise high. If you make a constant effort to make the sun rise, never resting or letting up, you will find a grand path opening up before you. In life, it is essential constantly to create firm foundations, become a person of higher caliber and create the graceful stability of an iceberg. Always work on enlarging your foundations, always strive to grow. If you hold to this attitude, you will find that a path to boundless development, a path to greatness of character, will open up before you.

Chapter Two

The Principle of Accumulation

1. The Significance of a Single Day

In this chapter, I would like to discuss how important it is to have an inner store of wisdom to create the stability of an iceberg in your life. First of all, I would like to consider the significance of a single day. Life is actually nothing more than a series or accumulation of single days. From ancient times, there have been various sayings about the significance of a single day, such as "Live each day as if it were your whole life," or as Jesus Christ said, "Therefore do not worry about tomorrow, for tomorrow will worry about itself. Each day has enough trouble of its own" (Matthew 6.34 NIV).

What kind of person you really are and the kind of life you have led will be revealed by the way you have lived each day and how each day has followed on from the one before. Human beings cannot borrow time from tomorrow nor can they take it from yesterday. You may be able to predict what will happen in the future, but you cannot make use of time that has yet to come. In the same way, although you may be able to reflect on what happened in the past, and learn lessons from it, you cannot change it. The only time that you are free to use is the time we are experiencing in this moment.

Because of this, each day holds an important key to successful living. Sooner or later, everyone will leave this world; some will go to heaven and some will go to hell and it is the accumulation of your days on Earth that decides where you will go. The sum total of the way you have lived each day will determine what kind of world you will go to after death, so you should be careful not to treat even a single day lightly.

As for the way you should spend each day, what is important is how to control and increase its quality. You cannot change the length of one day; it lasts twenty-four hours and there is no way it can be extended. However, it is possible for you to change the quality.

In a sense, scientific technology has been of great service in improving the quality of our days. For instance, calculations that used to take several days can now be done in a relatively short time with the use of computers. Insofar as technology has shortened time, we can say that we have succeeded in increasing the quality of each day. It cannot be denied that advances in technology have resulted in a more efficient use of time, but it is also possible to alter the quality of each day by means of our spiritual perspective and our state of mind.

The majority of people spend their lives with some kind of worry or emotional pain and the way they deal with this will affect their whole life. In other words, it is possible for people who have a higher level of awareness to cut through their worries or suffering in a single stroke. For example, if you devote yourself to spiritual refinement every day and keep your mind calm, you will not be overly affected no matter what happens in the outside world and you will be able to lead your life tranquilly.

If, on the other hand, you are caught up in the whirlpool of a busy life, at times you may be seized by worries that cause you to lose yourself. For example, those who deal with the stock market may at times fall into the trap of believing that following the prices of shares every day, every hour or even every minute is all that matters. As a result, they experience great pain if their stocks plunge in value. In contrast, however, seekers of Truth have no such worries and meditate calmly. This difference arises because of the different state of mind.

In the workplace, you may suffer because a colleague has been promoted ahead of you, because you have been told off by your boss for a mistake you made, or because you did not make as much profit as you expected. However, these are by no means serious problems for those whose state of mind is purer. A problem that occupies most of your thoughts during the day can easily be settled if you look at it from a higher point of view. If you have been worrying for a week or a month about a problem that could be solved in just three minutes by someone who can see it from a higher perspective, this means you are wasting your life away.

Each day is very precious, so you should give more thought to the state of mind you need to maintain throughout your day. You cannot increase the length of a day but you can improve the quality of it, so I would like you to think about how much and what kind of effort you need to make to do this. Try to find the magic that changes life into gold, try to find a way to make each of your days glow brightly.

2. A Willingness to Learn

When considering the significance of a single day, you should examine how to improve the quality of the limited time it contains. What is important here is the aspiration to learn.

First, you can learn by gaining knowledge. As I explained in the last chapter, one of the keys to understanding life can be found in the thoughts of great figures. By reading books of ideologies, philosophy and literature, your mind will be lifted to a higher state and problems in your life can be solved quite easily. Accumulating knowledge is most important when trying to attain a higher level of awareness. The reason a higher level of awareness is important is that it means your spiritual level develops accordingly.

In fact, the greatness of a human being is determined by his or her awareness, that is to say, from how high or broad a perspective a person views others and this world. For instance, even a subject in which you need instruction from others can be easily mastered if you have accumulated a good foundation of information and knowledge in reserve.

Misunderstandings also happen in life, and the cause usually lies in a lack of awareness of others' feelings, or not understanding the reason that something has happened to you. It takes time to listen to the explanations of others, and sometimes you may not be able to avoid misunderstandings. Nevertheless, if you know about the lives and views of many different people, you will be able to understand why you find yourself in such a difficult situation. Accumulating knowledge will serve you greatly in understanding yourself, understanding others and understanding this world, that is to say the world created by God.

What will you acquire through a better understanding of yourself, others, and the world? The answer is happiness. Knowing is a joy for human beings. As you widen your sphere of understanding, your inner world, too, will become vaster.

I am sure that no one would want to be an ant. Why? It is a matter of the way in which we view the world. There is a big difference between the worldview of an ant and the worldview of a human being. Ants cannot think or understand in the same way human beings do. Because of this huge gulf in awareness, a human being wants to remain human and has no wish to become an ant. So knowing in and of itself is also a source of great happiness.

Learning is not necessarily the only means of acquiring knowledge; you can also learn from experience. To do this, you need to live each day in the belief that it contains something that will serve to enrich your life. When you are in the middle of life's storms, you tend to complain and ask yourself why you should have to suffer such pain or misfortune, but the fact is that there are certain lessons to learn in these circumstances. There is no doubt that they work as whetstones in life to refine the soul.

You may wish that you could live a calm life and that every day would pass peacefully, but imagine when you come to the end of your life. When you looked back over your entire life, if it had been ordinary and uneventful, do you think you would be able to say that you had had a good life and leave this world fulfilled? In actual fact, it is when you are struggling to overcome difficulties that your soul shines and your joy increases. Certainly you may have to endure hard times when you struggle with hardships and difficulties, but in these can be found the richness of life and you will grow in stature.

I have no intention of worshipping difficulties or distress, but it is an undeniable fact that these challenges work as catalysts for increasing human stature. If your life is merely ordinary, you will have no chances to grow. On the other hand, if you feel you are being torn apart by suffering, you will gain tremendous self-confidence by overcoming these struggles.

The secret of those whom others see as "wise" lies in their positive attitude, trying to learn and absorb as much as possible from each person and from every experience. There are any number of people in this world with one aspect of their being which is more advanced than the greatest saints. There can be no denying that Confucius was a great man, but there are people who can demonstrate marvelous expertise he never possessed. There are even things to be learned from those who are regarded as evil by society; among them are some who would not hesitate to do anything to help a friend in need.

In life, we are given an assignment by God—how much can we learn from our experiences? The more changes or ups and downs that there are in a life, the more seeds we have to learn from. Our challenge is how much we are able to learn from our experiences.

To conclude this section I would like to emphasize that you should become more and more eager to learn, and be proud of how much you have learned in a single day. It is fine to keep a diary but it should not just be a report of what has happened during the day. It is what you have learned that day that is important. Finding some positive meaning in suffering or worries is of much more value to the soul than simply passing each day without accumulating experience. Nothing in life is a waste if seen from the perspective that all experiences are nourishment for the soul.

3. The Effects of Accumulating Knowledge and Experience

So far I have discussed the significance of a single day and the importance of a willingness to learn; now I would like to talk about the effects of accumulating knowledge and experience.

In the last ten years, I have published hundreds of books and a lot of people have expressed their surprise at my having written so many books in such a short period of time. Without sufficient inner "stock," most people would run out of ideas long before they had written such a large number of books. In my case, however, the fountain of topics is not exhausted. Why is this? Because I take in more than I put out or, in other words, I fill myself more than I empty myself. There are people who are always expending energy and rarely recharge themselves, but they need to understand the principle that people cannot give out more than the "stock" they have accumulated. For this reason it is very important to increase your stock of knowledge and experience.

This applies not only mentally and intellectually but also financially. In family finances, you cannot spend more than you earn unless you have savings. This is why those who are wise spend within the limits of their income, and save a part of it. This is a sensible way of living.

Today, people use credit cards and many bask in the benefits of our "credit card society." It seems that a lot of people enjoy living on credit, purchasing with ease electrical appliances or cars that they would find difficult to buy with cash. I admit these cards are useful, but you should not base your life on loans. The idea of using money in advance, anticipating future income, is not a heavenly but a negative way of thinking, which does not always accord with the Truth. God appreciates a steady way of life, when you live within your income and accumulate savings.

There are some who have started a crusade against credit cards because so many people are unable to control their spending. I have heard there are even people who make a living out of cutting credit cards into little pieces and throwing them away for those who cannot do it themselves. Some people own a number of different credit cards and overuse them, then find themselves deeply in debt and take out a loan to pay off a previous loan; in this way, the total amount of money they have borrowed grows larger and larger. Even then, they still cannot throw away their credit cards. This is why they get others to destroy the cards so they can finally escape their nightmare of loans. This example illustrates human weakness. I would like you to live within the limits of your income and set aside savings for the future.

The same principles apply to human souls. People tend to want to be superior to those around them, so they strive for titles and positions even when they do not have the necessary skills or abilities. This attitude is wrong, because guiding people before you have accumulated sufficient abilities is the same as spending your bonus in advance and charging up purchases to your credit card.

Although everyone would like to be president of a company, this is simply not possible. If someone who has accumulated sufficient skills and experience becomes president, he or she has much to offer and this brings benefits for many. If, on the other hand, someone who does not have sufficient skills or experience becomes president, he or she will not do a good job and, as a result, will bring suffering to other people involved.

The same holds true for actors and sports players whose popularity exceeds their abilities. It is good to achieve the level of popularity appropriate to your ability, but if your popularity exceeds your ability, that popularity is only superficial. True fame and popularity accompany true ability. If you try to win greater popularity than your actual level of competence warrants, you will lose your footing.

So, it is important to accumulate the resources to be successful in life. Even if these resources are not used or appreciated in this lifetime, they will be stored up in your treasure house in heaven. Although what you learn in this life may not help you at work or in your family life, the truth is that nothing you learn on this Earth is ever wasted. In school you may have studied physics, chemistry or geography and wondered whether these subjects would be useful in the future. However, they are all material for balancing your awareness. This phenomenon may be called "unnecessary necessity."

No matter how large a bridge may be, it only needs to be about a foot wide for a person to be able to walk across it. However, this is not to say that the rest of the bridge is useless. Suppose there was a log bridge one foot wide over a fast-flowing stream; most people would be afraid of the swift current below and be unable to cross. The same is true of walking a tightrope. If the rope is on the ground, anyone can walk along it, but if people see someone walking it when it is between two roofs, they are impressed and think they could never do the same.

Similarly, there is always a part of you that, although it is not used, actually serves to protect you from various dangers and keeps your mind steady. This is what I mean by "unnecessary necessity." It is this inner accumulation that constitutes your true ability. If you have not accumu lated much, you are likely to be swayed by small things, whereas if you have accumulated a great deal within and have great self-confidence you will not be easily swayed by unfavorable criticism or setbacks. For this reason, it is important to accumulate sufficient knowledge and experi- ence, which together become like the part of an iceberg that is beneath the surface.

Inner accumulation has another surprising effect; it will unexpectedly provide the key to opening up your life.

Even if your store of knowledge does not seem to be of any use now, in ten or twenty years it may bloom in a way that you could never have imagined. It is not easy to know what you will need in the future; although you may feel you have had many unnecessary experiences, perhaps they will serve you in times to come.

For myself, before I started on the path of religion, I worked for six years in a general trading company. While I was working there, the question always arose, why should I spend most of my time each day working in a field that had nothing to do with the Truth or spiritual subjects? Again and again the thought crossed my mind that this work could not be my true purpose in life.

My job in the company was dealing with foreign exchange, international finance and domestic funds, so I had a good understanding of the way in which money flowed. At the same time, I thought the financial field had nothing to do with the world of the mind, and I had a vague sense of anxiety about the direction my life was taking. However, I realize now that those experiences have stood me in good stead at IRH, the Institute for Research in Human Happiness. During my time at the trading company, I learned about people, how to manage an organization, how money flows, how to make efficient use of funds, etc. and all these things have been useful in my present work.

Many of those who intend to accomplish something in the spiritual arena seem to lack the skills of organizational management and putting money to good use. Many religious leaders in particular are ignorant of these sorts of practical matters. Lacking knowledge and experience, they fail to manage groups and ultimately fail to accomplish their main purpose or fulfill their original intention. However, because I made the utmost effort in fields that seemed to have nothing to do with the Truth, in other words I accumulated what seemed unnecessary, I have an inner store of knowledge and experience. I actually feel that this now helps me in different ways.

During my time at the trading company, I also had the chance to work in the United States with people from all over the world, not only Americans but also Koreans, Chinese and Filipinos. This experience gave me the opportunity to get to know the characteristics and ways of thinking of people from many other countries, and exposed me to values that were different from my own.

Today, I teach the diversity of Truth and the diversity of what is right. If I search for the origins of this teaching, I can say that in part they are to be found in my experiences of international society, where I had the chance to get to know many different people with many different ways of thinking. I learned that there are numerous ways of thinking besides my own that are reasonable and this influenced my current thinking on diversity.

There are many religious leaders with different teachings, yet all insist that their particular creed is the only true one. The reason I am free of this sort of thinking is that I have worked with people of many nationalities and races, and absorbed many of their ways of thinking. This store of knowledge serves as "unnecessary necessity" for me.

Therefore, people can learn many things through their jobs. Even if you are now engaged in something that seems far from useful in terms of your aims for the future, it may be serving you in some way. You may feel that you are doing something irrelevant or that you are taking the long way round in reaching your aim or ideal. But it is important to make the best use of the materials you are now being given.

If you keep on solving the problems you are presented with, in due course this will serve you in some way. Even if you feel that the mathematics you studied at school has been of very little use to you since you graduated, your learning serves to provide a sense of balance for your character and your store of knowledge. To use another example, it is not enough for a novelist just to read works of literature. A writer needs to know about the world and the changes taking place in society to support his or her work.

To create an inner store of knowledge, it is important not to limit your studies to what you need to know right now but rather to take an interest in a wide range of subjects and continue collecting information. Even if it is not useful for you at present, accumulating knowledge that you feel may come in useful at some time in the future will be of great benefit to you some day.

4. An Unexpected Harvest

In the previous section, I explained that as a result of accumulating knowledge and experience, you will reap an unexpected harvest. Sometimes it happens in this lifetime, sometimes in the next. It is not unusual to find that people who seemed quite miserable on this Earth achieve a wonderful state after death in the other world. It also happens that people of no particular standing while living on this Earth reach a surprisingly high level in the other world.

Mary, who gave birth to Jesus, had a pure heart and lived an ordinary life as a carpenter's wife. She loved Jesus as her own son, rather than as a distant being or a savior. When, at the age of thirty, Jesus started teaching people about the path to God, he attracted many to him but he was also persecuted. Throughout her life, Mary was concerned for the happiness of her beloved son. On witnessing Jesus' crucifixion, she fell into deep sorrow.

In her lifetime, Mary never thought of herself as someone special. However, since leaving this world and returning to a place corresponding to her high spiritual level, she has become known as the Virgin Mary, one of the most revered women on Earth. Now, she listens to the worries of many and works hard on behalf of people all over the world, especially women and children, and families.

On Earth, Mary lived an ordinary life, the life of a carpenter's wife. It was an honest life. She never expected to become someone special after death. She treated her husband, children and neighbors with great kindness and lived with faith. She was not concerned with worldly status, fame or honor, and it is an undeniable fact that she loved her son Jesus with her whole heart. After leaving this world, people like this reap their "harvest" accordingly. It is said that even if you do not seek divine favor, it will be given to you, and this is the truth that the story of Mary reveals.

Although you need to accumulate different experiences in life and build up an inner store, you should not seek only good outcomes. Do not be too concerned with results. Life is full of unexpected harvests and sudden reversals. It is possible that someone such as a Prime Minister or President who has been respected in this world may not be able to return to heaven, while someone who has led an ordinary life may go to a very high level in the heavenly world. The criteria that determine where you go after death are clarity, purity of mind and selflessness. For those who possess these traits, everything becomes material for learning, leading them along the path to self-development.

To reap an unexpected harvest, you must strive to live sincerely, with a pure heart. If you live sincerely, you may sometimes face situations in this world where you are laughed at or misunderstood. However, at some point in time, your attitude of living wholeheartedly and your purity of heart will yield an abundant harvest.

Through my many books I have revealed the truth about the world of thought and the actual existence of a spirit world. But not everyone can understand these things; some misunderstand. However, as long as I swear that I am not telling lies and I speak with a pure heart, I believe it is important to keep on teaching the Truth as it is. I believe that sooner or later people will come to understand.

Now, I am filled with the determination to publish as many books of Truth as possible, books about the Truth and about the mind. I hope my writings will help people even in some small way to open up a new life. I will be happy if these books help people find happiness and nourishment for their souls, not only those people who read them now but also those who will be born after I have left this world. This is my wish.

You should not accumulate knowledge and experience for the purpose of fulfilling selfish desires or satisfying your own interests. It is essential to accumulate wisdom day by day, with a pure wish to be of service to the divine in times to come. This is the true meaning of "storing up treasure in heaven." Do not look for the approval of others in this world or the next. It is important to live with a pure heart, to tell people what you believe and never let things be left in a way that you will later regret.

5. The Path to Re-creating Happiness

I would like to finish this chapter by discussing "the path to re-creating happiness." Human beings gain many different kinds of knowledge during the course of their lives; they also learn a lot from their numerous experiences. This learning is not just for themselves, nor is it simply for its own sake. For example, the money you earn through working will be worth nothing if you simply leave it behind. Only when you use it does it have any meaning. In using money, you will circulate it, so that what you earn can become others' income.

The same can be said of experiences. What you experience or realize through things that happen should not be just for your own satisfaction. It is important to pass on what you have learned to help others become more enlightened. In your lifetime, you will probably learn many lessons. Instead of storing these lessons up just for yourself, you should pass them on to society in different forms. You can share them with your family, with your friends and with the many people you encounter in your life.

First, you need to become more enlightened day by day. Then you will be able to lead others to higher enlightenment from your own "stock." It is important not only to share enlightenment in ways that are visible. I teach of "existence as love,"[1] and you should be aware that the very existence of a person who has acquired much knowledge, learned lessons and attained a higher level of enlightenment is an expression of great love for others.

1. Refer to *The Laws of the Sun* by Ryuho Okawa (Lantern Books, 2001), Chapter Three: The River of Love.

If there is one single person in a company who has attained a high level of enlightenment through learning life's lessons, he or she will be a great source of love to those who work in the same place. Imagine what great love this person represents, as an embodiment of "existence as love."

For those who seek Dharma, or the Truth, how blessed it is that there is a teacher! Money cannot buy this. The existence of Buddha, Jesus, Confucius and Socrates was invaluable to those who were living in the same age. The Chinese Buddhist philosopher T'ien-t'ai Chih-i (538–597) said, "I wish to be reborn at the time of the rebirth of Buddha. I would not even mind being a leper, as long as I could be alive then." What he says is very true. The mere existence of someone who has attained great enlightenment and become a great teacher brings happiness to those who are living at the same time.

Not everyone is able to preach the Dharma, but even the smallest of beings is capable of emitting the light of enlightenment. Everyone is capable of becoming a little "giant of love." As well as accumulating experiences in the course of your life, you should use what you have accumulated for the joy and happiness of others. Once you have attained happiness, re-create it for the benefit of others. This is the task that human beings have been set. I would like you to visualize "re-creating happiness" and strive to accumulate an inner store.

CHAPTER THREE

Confronting Anxiety and Distress

1. Different Aspects of Distress

When considering how to live happily, everything comes back to how you confront the suffering that you face in the course of your life. Life is like a workbook of problems to be solved, and each of you is given challenges that are appropriate for your soul. It is the way in which you overcome these trials that reveals your true nature. The suffering you experience in life shows you clearly what kind of spiritual training you are going through and what is most important for you.

The word "distress" brings to mind an image of the life of the composer Beethoven. Imagine the suffering he must have endured, continuing to compose music while he was losing his hearing. No one would want a life as difficult as Beethoven's, but he was a man who always gave of his utmost and whose soul undoubtedly gave out light.

More recently, we have the example of Helen Keller. If we were to compare Helen Keller to Napoleon or

Goethe, it would not be easy to say who was of greater stature. There were probably few nights when the Emperor Napoleon was able to sleep peacefully. Similarly the great writer and statesman Goethe seemed to have many sleepless nights. He said that the number of days of real happiness in his whole life would not add up to more than one month.

Why is Helen Keller's life considered as admirable as the lives of other great figures? I would say it is because of her attitude; despite the great adversities she suffered, she made a constant effort to find the wonder in everything. When people are healthy and their lives flow smoothly, they have a tendency to look at what is lacking. However, if they were to find themselves unable to see or hear or speak, all that would be left would be the fact of being alive. It is important to realize that the very fact of being given life is amazing.

I have heard that sometimes people who have lost their sight dream only in sounds, and always in darkness. But they are still alive and even in such adverse circumstances they are able to grasp the true meaning of life. From time to time, you need to look at yourself and learn from the examples of those who lived through great hardship.

What is the cause of your suffering? In many cases, it is some trifling, emotional conflict. Perhaps you often compare yourself with others, and experience pain recognizing a gap that exists. The cause of most suffering is conflict with others. However, you will never be able to free yourself of suffering as long as you compare yourself to others, because if you look back at your past or look around you, there is always someone to envy. This is true for everyone.

In ancient Greece, there was a philosopher named Diogenes. It is said he always dressed in rags and lived in a large tub; he was known as "the sage in the tub." One day, Alexander the Great visited the town and on meeting Diogenes announced, "Tell me what you desire and I will grant your wish." However, Diogenes merely said, "Please stand out of the way, you're blocking the sunlight." This story has been handed down for over 2,000 years.

Happiness for Diogenes was a quiet life, basking in the sun in his tub. He enjoyed peace of mind and needed nothing more than this. He was satisfied just to bathe in the sun; he never had the slightest desire for fine clothes or money, status, fame, or anything else. All he wanted was to sit in his tub and think, free to do exactly as he wanted without anyone else telling him what to do. Then Alexander the Great, in whom Diogenes had not the slightest interest, arrived and stood in front of him, blocking the sunlight. When Diogenes asked Alexander to stand out of his light, Alexander the Great was speechless.

Alexander believed that there was nothing in the world that did not come under his dominion. Certainly, he had the power to fulfill any worldly desire; he could grant any wish for a palace, money and wives. Yet, in spite of the fact that Alexander the Great possessed such powers, to

Diogenes he was no more than an obstruction, blocking the sunlight and throwing him into shadow. This episode illustrates the difference between someone who inhabits the kingdom within and someone who lives for the glory of the material world.

There is a similar anecdote from ancient China. One of the most famous Chinese philosophers of the hundred schools period, Chuang-tzu (367–279 B.C.), had a similar experience. When he was offered the post of Prime Minister, he turned it down instantly. The story goes that he said he would rather frolic in the mud like a pig than live a suffocating life of service. Worldly status had absolutely no meaning for him.

In the replies of Diogenes and Chuang-tzu I see two men who were perfect sovereigns in their own kingdom of the mind and who were not swayed by the circumstances around them or worldly values. One man was happy without wanting any of the power, fame or money that Alexander the Great could give; the other wanted to frolic in the mud like a pig rather than hold a ministerial post. Neither of these men would allow their happiness to be influenced by the words or opinions of others, or by circumstances others created; they were great men because they were rulers of their own kingdom within.

When I look at the different kinds of distress that exist, I see the cause of our suffering lies in the fact that we are constantly comparing ourselves with others. We create suffering by trying to adjust ourselves to outside values, for example, by being swayed by the words of others, and by becoming confused by the enormous amounts of information that our eyes and ears absorb.

Sometimes you would do well to remember the stories of Diogenes and Chuang-tzu, and look at your suffering afresh, from the perspective that you may be trying to attain happiness by imposing outside values on your inner world. Are you sure that you are completely in charge of the kingdom of the mind? If you compare your state of mind to that of Diogenes or Chuang-tzu, are you strong enough, not easily swayed by worldly considerations such as money, status or the opposite sex? You need to examine whether the cause of your suffering could actually be trying to seek happiness outside of yourself.

2. Anxiety in Life

The origins of most anxieties in life are to be found in a person's sense of values. Anxiety usually stems from a fear that you will be held in lower regard by others than you would wish. For instance, when you fall in love, you are scared that you will be rejected; when you start working for a company, you are worried you will never get a good position; when you launch a business, you are afraid that it will go bankrupt, or that you will fall sick. Anxieties like these all stem from worries that things will be worse than they are at present. So, the fundamental cause of distress or anxiety in life is the belief that your happiness is dependent on outside factors; this makes the mind waver.

I would now like to talk about the story of Job, which appears in the Old Testament. Job, a good and righteous man, possessed a strong faith and no matter what happened, it never wavered. However, there came a time when Job suffered one misfortune after another. His cattle died, his servants were murdered, and his sons and daughters died in accidents. As if that was not enough, swellings appeared all over his body and he became completely miserable. With all these misfortunes, Job lost everything he possessed.

He finally began to express his anguish as to why he had to suffer so many misfortunes, although he had lived his life with faith. He believed that pious people should be rewarded accordingly and that they deserved success, prosperity and glory. He questioned why his family had been taken from him, why his cattle had died, and why he had become disfigured by the swellings all over his body. God answered, asking Job how much he knew of the workings of heaven and the thoughts of the creator of the universe. God also asked if Job understood the true significance of the ordeals that had befallen him. Job was wrong in cursing the circumstances he had been given.

In short, what the Old Testament is trying to teach here is that you will not attain happiness by railing against your circumstances. If you believe in God only when things are going well but not when things become difficult, your faith is not genuine. Faith is within. Nothing from outside of you can destroy it. No matter if you are about to be crucified, shot or crushed by a tank, it is important that you defend the kingdom within. You may be criticized or abused by others; this may be the equivalent of bullets. However, you need to have an unshakable belief, a faith that will not be swayed even if you are hit by those bullets.

When everything was going well, Job believed earnestly in God. However, when he was beset by misfortune, he began to lose his faith. You can see numerous examples of this in daily life. For instance, you may trust someone who has treated you well but as soon as the situation changes for the worse, you lose your trust in that person.

The same thing can happen at the office. As long as your boss is helping you to get ahead, you work hard for him, but the moment you feel he has withdrawn his support, you may start to criticize him. Ordinary people usually behave like this. In religious groups, too, the same thing happens. When people are given an important role they work hard, but as soon as the role is taken away, they start to complain. This attitude is the height of folly.

These people find themselves in the same situation as Job. When your circumstances are favorable it is not difficult to live in accordance with faith; it is in deep adversity that faith is tested. In some cases, God sends human beings ordeals to temper their souls. The soul is strengthened in both good fortune and adversity, and it is through these two extremes that your true nature is revealed. God requires that human beings do not become conceited in good fortune, and that they do not fall into deep despair when they experience misfortune. Rather, He expects us to keep making a steady effort in every situation.

All anxiety in life originates from the concern that your standing will be diminished in relation to others. You begin to question whether your strengths are as positive as you thought. Suppose a woman feels that her beauty is the sole source of her happiness. When her beauty fades, what will be left? What about a man who regards his youth as the only quality he values in himself? When he loses his youth, what will happen?

Here I am trying to illustrate the true nature of anxiety. You writhe in agony, unable to endure situations where something from outside seems about to hurt you or to reduce your worth. At these times, you need to be aware that your faith and conviction are being tested. If you only believe in God when everything is going well and do not believe in Him in unfavorable situations, it means that your faith is not real, and you are only looking for the advantages faith can bring.

So be aware that most anxieties in life stem from an attitude of searching for the seeds of happiness in the outside world. Worries arise when you have not succeeded in taking responsibility for your inner self, when it is not yet strong enough.

3. On Sleepless Nights

Most people have probably experienced sleepless nights when they toss and turn, distressed amid life's worries.

Some of you may be having restless nights at the moment. You lie awake in bed and gaze into the darkness, unable to get a wink of sleep as you wait for the day to dawn. Just as you are on the verge of dozing off, it is time to get up. You have to go to work, but you are in bad shape and in a bad mood, and feel distinctly unhappy. You have probably experienced this kind of a day.

How can you cope with a sleepless night? Usually the cause of loss of sleep is worry. For those who suffer sleepless nights, I would like to point out the following facts. First, sleepless nights do not continue for very long. No one ever has difficulty sleeping for as long as three or four years—it is only a temporary condition. Another fact is that your soul is being tempered at this time. What is important is the extent to which you forge and temper your soul to refine it at these times.

If you are constantly lying awake at night, instead of making any hasty decisions about what to do, you need to endure this time. There is a theory that in life, there are seven-year cycles. According to the Japanese statesman Katsu Kaishu (1823–1899), life cycles change every seven to ten years, so if you stand in the shade for ten years, you will eventually see the sun again. On the other hand, although the sun may be shining on you now, in another ten years you may experience the shade. The tides of destiny do not flow in the same direction for more than ten years.

This is quite possible. Just because the sun is not shining on you, there is very little to be gained by wailing, lamenting and complaining about it. People are calmly watching to see how you lead your life in the face of adversity. If you behave in the same way that people who suffer misfortune usually do, you will learn nothing from the experience and, as a result, others will not hold you in very high regard. How you lead your life when you are going through adversity is very important.

If we were to classify human beings into levels, those who moan, complain or get angry in misfortune could be regarded as belonging to the lowest category. Those who quietly endure sorrow or pain fall into the middle category, while those who try to get over their immediate problem and better themselves could be classified as lower-end of the high level. Those in the moderately high category are aware that they should make the utmost effort in the face of adversity while those at the highest level try to find some positive meaning in a difficult situation and learn lessons to further strengthen their souls. It is important to train yourself to be strong instead of holding on to misfortune for a long time.

I remember once reading a story about a child who was physically weak and was told that when he grew up he would not have good health. He decided that he would somehow overcome this weakness, so from childhood he regularly went running along the bank of a river. In the end, he was selected to represent his country at the Olympics. This is how life works. Even if you think that you are below average at something, if you continue to work steadily on yourself instead of complaining or merely enduring, you will leap to an unexpectedly high level.

There are people who make an effort to improve themselves but hold on to their misfortunes, thinking how unhappy they are and that somehow they must escape their unhappiness. On the other hand, there are those who continue to strengthen and improve themselves steadily every day, not caring about their misfortune. The difference between the two is vast.

On sleepless nights, it is important to concentrate on making an effort to improve yourself. If you cannot sleep, it simply means you have more time to do things. When I have experienced sleepless nights, I have not forced myself to try to get some sleep; I have spent most of the time reading. When you are in the midst of difficulties, worries or anxieties, it will definitely not be a waste to spend the time developing and improving yourself. If I had been an athlete, perhaps I would have trained my physical body by running marathons. However, I was not that type; my interest was in the world of the mind and the world of thoughts so I trained myself in this field of study.

I started to communicate with the spirit world when I was twenty-four years old, yet it was not until I was thirty that I stood up and began to teach the Truth. For six years, I quietly continued developing my inner strength, waiting for the right time to come. During that period, I could have worried endlessly had I wanted to, because although I was experiencing spiritual phenomena and had a clear mission to carry out, I could not start out on my new path nor had a suitable environment manifested around me.

However, I did not spend my time worrying but instead led a busy life. I was determined to work harder than anyone else and to create an above average record at my company, while at the same time I was dedicating all my time outside work to investing in my future. I am now engaged in my true mission and looking back at my past I feel proud of my attitude and the fact that I concentrated on developing myself rather than struggling in vain.

If, at that time, I had spent my days worrying about how my situation had not changed despite the fact that I had received messages from high spirits and had realized the greatness of my mission, I might not be the same person I am today. However, during that time, I thought about my future. "What do I need to do? In the near future, I will have to give talks in front of large numbers of people and write books. For that, it will be essential to have refined myself spiritually and to have a store of knowledge. It will take four, five, maybe six decades to learn all the many lessons I need through experience, so I must back up my lack of experience with knowledge." With this thinking, I concentrated on developing myself. I had no doubt that sooner or later the appropriate circumstances would be given to me, so I just kept on developing myself further without worrying.

This is one way of coping with sleepless nights. Instead of complaining that you have not been provided with the circumstances suitable for your mission, you should tell yourself that if you really have a mission, then the appropriate circumstances will be given to you at the appropriate time, and that you will blossom according to your potential. You have no way of knowing when this will be; until then you should improve yourself tirelessly, focusing on what you think will be required of you. Without self-pity or sadness, you should build up your strength. Those who are easily swayed when they face difficulties are ordinary. At these times, it is important to make ceaseless and diligent efforts.

4. The Sun Also Rises

The expression "the sun also rises" may be old, but it describes one of life's truths; there is no doubt that the sun will rise again. Every evening, the sun disappears below the horizon and rises again without fail after about ten hours of darkness. The sun promises that after it has sunk it will certainly rise again.

I wonder if there is anyone in the whole world who imagines the sun will not come up. I am sure everyone believes that the sun will rise again; no one ever doubts it. Why? Because the sun came up this morning, yesterday morning, the day before yesterday, and last year. It rose ten years ago and even when our ancestors were living, so there is no reason to doubt that it will come up tomorrow too, and the day after.

The same holds true in life. After any hardship or difficulty, you can be sure that the sun will rise again. When you are experiencing some difficulty or suffering, I would strongly recommend that you look calmly at yourself from the perspective of a third person, and consider whether or not anyone else has ever faced the same problem. People tend to think their own worries are huge and that there is nothing they can do to solve them, but most problems are not unique. Similar problems have usually occurred before in the past, and they are occurring now as well. In most cases, other people have experienced distress or suffering similar to yours.

In connection with this subject, let me tell you an interesting fact. There are always people who are proud that they are suffering from a serious illness. If they go to the doctor and are told that it is nothing to worry about, they are not satisfied with the diagnosis and will go to another hospital. If they are told the same thing again, they will go on to the next hospital. Only when they have been told that their condition is very serious are they finally satisfied. There are numerous patients like this and, surprisingly, there are also many people who are relieved to be told their illness is unique.

In the field of psychiatry, quite a number of cases like this have been brought to light. There are many instances of patients who argue with their doctor. In many cases patients go to a psychiatrist to be diagnosed as having a complicated personality, as opposed to finding solutions to their problems. As a result of the difficulties they experience, bothering their psychotherapist actually becomes their way of enjoying a distorted sense of superiority; they want their therapists to acknowledge what complex and sensitive people they are.

Apart from psychiatrists and patients, there are many instances of similar sorts of problems in other relationships. I would like you to check and see whether you are trying to satisfy something in yourself by worrying and suffering. Are you sure that, having failed to win approval out in the world, you are not trying to make yourself into a tragic hero? Can you honestly say that you are not simply pretending to suffer anxiety out of a desire to be recognized as complex and sensitive? These are the questions you need to ask yourself.

There are people who always think the worst about their health and other problems, thus aggravating their worries. But at some point in life, they need to stop this tendency. Many people take a secret pleasure in the idea that they are miserable and deserve pity. They complain in many different ways, for instance: "I am unhappy because of this illness," "If only I had got a better score in the exam, my life would be better today," "The environment I was living in at that time resulted in my present situation," "If only that had not happened," or "If only things had been different."

This is called self-pity. Because people who pity themselves feel that others do not love them, they try hard to provide love for themselves. Although they may think that in doing so they are supplying themselves with "fertilizer," unfortunately this fertilizer contains poison. If they continue to supply this, sooner or later the "flowers" will wither. Self-pity is poisonous in the sense that it thwarts straightforward spiritual growth.

As long as people love themselves in a self-pitying way, they will not be blessed with qualities that are admired, nor will they add richness to their lives. Many people have a tendency to search for the slightest excuse to drive themselves into a corner, set themselves up as tragic heroes and then take pleasure in their own wounds. These people need to be aware that self-pity never leads to true happiness.

For instance, there are people who suffer for years from a broken heart. They may think that their partner was a wonderful person, and although they did everything they could for that person, their love was not rewarded. They remain broken-hearted for four or five years, believing there is no cure. Although they may believe the person they loved to be one of the most beautiful women or the most handsome men in the world, in most cases, the object of their love appears quite ordinary to someone close to that person.

Even popular actors and actresses look quite ordinary to their families, who do not regard them as particularly attractive. No matter how amazing they may appear to be on TV or in movies, in their private lives they are mostly just ordinary women wearing beautiful make-up or ordinary men who are no different from men you find anywhere else. In most cases, these "stars" do not think of themselves as extraordinary nor do they have high self-esteem.

Normally, people tend to idealize others on a whim, are hurt by their own obsession and get caught up in self-pity. For example, the woman you idealize may not be a great beauty, the like of whom you will never find again anywhere in the world. She is usually just someone who happens to have been in the same class or the same office as you, or someone you met on some other occasion. She is just one of a limited number of women who happens to match your ideal, and your assessment is not necessarily objective. The root of the tragedy lies in your arbitrary judgment that this woman is a peerless beauty.

To conclude, the key for the sun to rise again is not trying to hold on to the night for too long. It is important to know that the night will pass. In fact, you should free yourself from feelings of self-pity as soon as possible, and cast off the negative idea that you have been abandoned by this world. Always be conscious that you are a magnificent child of God and continue to move forward with this awareness as a support in life.

Though one person may criticize, another will praise you. Even if you cannot tell which opinion is true, just keep on moving forward. Only when the lid of your coffin has been closed will others understand clearly what kind of person you really were, so do not be upset by what others say at any one moment in time. I am not telling you to live an egotistical life; I am simply saying that it is not always possible for other people to understand you.

It is a fact that those who indulge in self-pity and who have a tendency to be tragic heroes often find themselves in tragic environments, just as those who disparage themselves often become targets of abuse. The same thing happens with dogs. People avoid throwing stones at or hitting a dog that looks strong, but a dog that looks ready to run away at the slightest threat may become a target of abuse. This perversity is part of human nature. For this reason, it is important that you do not let yourself appear weak.

Never indulge in self-pity; instead, walk your own path calmly and steadily. This is the secret of how to make the sun rise again.

5. Take Steady Steps

I would like to finish this chapter on confronting anxiety and distress by talking about the importance of taking steady steps. In times of distress, your mind will be swayed like a leaf in the wind, and you will tend to see problems as extremely serious. At such times, it is important to remember two perspectives.

One is the macro-perspective, to see yourself as if from infinitely far away. If, in the midst of your suffering and confusion, you were to see yourself through the eyes of God, from His vast perspective, is what is happening really so grave? In most cases, it is simply the result of comparing yourself with just a few hundred, perhaps a few thousand people, for instance those at your company. You might be upset that your colleague got a bigger bonus or was promoted to a higher position before you. Perhaps the cause is family circumstances, maybe your wife has become ill.

It is important to ask yourself if your suffering is really so enormous or whether it is actually a small thing, a common occurrence that will pass in time. This overview, the ability to see yourself from an infinite distance, is essential for solving life's problems.

The other important perspective is the micro perspective, that is to say focusing on enriching each day. When misfortune strikes, some people start working desperately in a bid to be noticed by others. They may attempt to do something exceptional or begin to talk big. For instance, someone who is suffering a broken heart may suddenly start something new in an eagerness to show that he is unaffected, or a person who has failed to get a promotion may suddenly start to brag about his hobbies. In this way, there are people who, driven by pain, try hard to appear exceptional.

Most often, however, these people become filled with self-hatred and find themselves in even more pain three to six months later. So it is true that when you are going through a hard time, you should not react in a big way or do anything showy. It is not a good idea to try to start a major project or brag in front of others in reaction to pain. If you do, it will bring about an even worse outcome and make you hate yourself even more.

When you are in pain, do not make any dramatic moves to attract the attention of others. Instead of acting in a showy way, keep walking steadily on your own path. This micro-perspective is also important. Within the realm of your own abilities, try to transform yourself and become a better person; walk steadily along the path to self-improvement. Be indifferent to the eyes of others; devote yourself to developing your abilities twenty-four hours a day.

There are people working in companies who, having failed to carry out the job that was entrusted to them, feel tormented and suggest bigger projects. However, at times like this, these people have lost their mental and emotional balance, their batteries have gone dead and need recharging. To recharge, these people need to act in a moderate fashion and spend their time building up an inner store. If you fail at work, it is important not to embark on even bigger projects out of wounded pride, but instead to look calmly at yourself and cultivate the inner self for about six months.

What is most important is walking forward, taking steady steps each day. Keep a careful eye on your health and enrich your inner self. Whenever your eyes see something disturbing or your mind is swayed by something outside of you, direct your mind inward to create an inner store.

Just because war has broken out in a foreign country, there is no need to rush around with a spear in your hand. To build a nation that will not be disposed to war, you need to educate the people, construct a stable economy and create productive agriculture. In other words, you should establish firm foundations within. Whenever you are off guard, you are liable to attacks from outside, so do not leave any unguarded areas in your mind.

As I have explained, there are two main perspectives with which to confront anxiety and distress. One is to view any misfortune that occurs from a macro-perspective, that is to say, from the perspective of God. Then you may well become aware that your problem is not as big as you imagined, that it is a commonplace situation that will pass away sooner or later. The other perspective to see yourself from is the micro-perspective. It is not a good idea to talk big, plan major projects or take dramatic action to try to justify failure. If you do, you will be regarded as someone without much potential. In adversity, you should remain serene and continue developing yourself.

If you really are an important and competent member of society, you will not be pushed aside forever; you will eventually be noticed. I am not saying that you should wait for seven years for the cycle to pass. Within six months to a year, the day will come when you are reassessed and presented with a new position. In the meantime, it is important to be discreet in speech and action, and to refine the inner self. To confront and overcome anxiety and distress, you should walk steadily forward every day.

CHAPTER FOUR

Spiritual Influences As the Cause of Suffering

1. The Origin of Negative Spiritual Influences

When solving life's problems, it is very important to understand the negative influences of spiritual beings. People who believe in the existence of the spirit world may wonder about the existence of ghosts. Although people have heard of ghosts in fairy tales or horror stories, they do not imagine spirits having anything to do with their reality. In the unseen world, however, spirits that exert a negative influence are certainly active and they try to influence us in certain ways.

So what are these spirits? The best way to describe them is as spirits who are responsive to the negative energy emitted by human beings, that is to say the energy of people's negative thoughts. People who constantly have negative thoughts while they are alive on Earth go to the realm of hell after they die, and live there as stray spirits.[1]

---

1. Stray spirits can be described as confused, misguided, negative or even evil beings that have strayed from the path of Truth.

In other words, stray spirits were not originally created at the beginning of time; they are those who strayed from the right path in the process of living and it is possible for anyone to become a stray spirit.

As human beings, we have been granted the freedom to hold any thought we want in our minds, and by exercising this freedom we are able to change our very being. Through full use of this freedom of thought, people are able to turn themselves into either beings of good or beings of evil. Stray spirits are those who failed to use this freedom correctly.

Where did they go wrong? I would like to look closely at this point. The reason people become stray spirits is they have generated thoughts that hurt others. An attitude of loving oneself is not wrong, but it is an undeniable fact that self-love contains feelings of either active or passive ill-will toward others. Within the egocentric mindset is the wish to pull other people down or the wish to be number one.

If applied correctly, the wish to value oneself can accord with the principles of development and prosperity. However, if this is even slightly misused, it will cause a great number of negative consequences. For example, if you think only of yourself, you will not mind about the consequences of throwing garbage into a river; you will not care that it creates problems for the people living downstream. For this reason there are specific rules for garbage disposal. If you were only concerned about keeping the inside of your own house clean, you could easily toss your garbage out onto the street, but this is not permitted. Those who cannot understand why this is not allowed will not be liked.

Whether or not individuals are able to understand such rules is what demonstrates their humanity, because the fundamental challenge of being human is how to live as an individual while at the same time living in harmony with the whole of society. As an individual, each person needs to manifest his or her own uniqueness and distinctive qualities but, at the same time, the individual needs to create harmony and contribute to the development of the whole.

Here is the origin of stray spirits. As a result of the conflict between the freedom of individuals, negativity is created in the form of distortion, and stray spirits embody this negativity in the course of their lives and live based on it. Humans are spiritual beings, and their thoughts reveal their true nature. Trying to attribute the cause of misfortune to the environment or to other people is the reason negativity arises. You should consider the correct way—or a better way—to live as a human being, from the point of view of governing your inner self. Although it is difficult to change your environment, you can always change your thoughts.

About two thousand years ago, three men were crucified on a hill in Golgotha in what is now Israel. Two of them were criminals, murderers and thieves; the other was a prisoner who was contemptuously called "King of the

Jews," whose crime was to declare himself this. He was
Jesus Christ. Although the objective fact of the crucifixion
of each of these three men was the same, there was a
world of difference between Jesus' state of mind and the
state of mind of the other two men.

No matter what circumstances you are placed in, you
are given complete control over the government of your
own mind. So the thoughts that are in your mind during
the course of your life are very important. In fact, the
reason that stray spirits come into being is that they have
misused the freedom they were blessed with.

While a fruit knife can be used to peel fruit, it can also
be used to injure others. The knife does not come with
instructions that it should only be used to peel fruit and not
to hurt others; this is left to the common sense of the individual. In short, good and evil arise out of the process of
exercising our freedom, which is the most precious gift
that human beings are given. If there were a mechanism to
prevent the generation of all negative thoughts in the
human mind, we would lose our freedom. As a result, the
exquisite beauty of life and the material for spiritual
development would no longer exist.

Seen from a higher perspective, negativity is an effective tool in assisting the development of the soul. To
become a stray spirit is the pitiable result of misuse of the
freedom of the soul.

2. Misguided Religions

I would now like to look at the different kinds of stray spirits that exist. First, there are spirits that are connected with certain religions. These spirits make their way into misguided religions and influence the minds of those who gather there.

Today, a large number of religious groups exist and many people are associated with them in one way or another. Among them are many misguided organizations where evil has found a way into the founder or the teachings, and misleads their followers. Large numbers of spirits inhabit these kinds of religious organizations. What is the cause of this type of spirit appearing in the world?

There are a lot of spirits in hell who want to be saved, and they are always searching for ways to lessen their pain and distress. They are waiting for someone to eliminate their suffering and bring them relief. If these spirits go to misguided religious organizations and possess the people there, they can temporarily escape their sufferings of hell. For this reason, large numbers of spirits gather around these groups. It often happens that followers who previously did not have any particular troubles will experience disharmony in the home because they have become involved with a misguided religion and are being negatively influenced by spirits. In this way, the presence of stray spirits is increased in this world.

As well as these spirits, there are other particularly malign spirits, who are also described as "devils" or "satanic." These beings struggle to take over even good religions and so hinder the work of Angels of Light. They are always on the lookout for opportunities within a religion to spread confusion and cause it to break up into small factions. Approaches from these malign spirits are a common occurrence in religious organizations. Religion is essentially marvelous, but sometimes these obstructions create confusion. Such beings are filled with frustration and they are trying somehow to achieve self-realization. However, their self-realization takes the form of the destruction, of trying to ruin others.

Taking pleasure in watching other people's ruin and suffering is the worst mental attitude possible for a human being. Malign beings thrive at this level. The human mind is capable of highs and lows, and at its very lowest state it derives pleasure from seeing the misfortune of others, laughing scornfully and wishing to cause even further unhappiness.

Spirits that are connected to certain religions possess people through this darkness. They will possess someone who is overwhelmed by worries and desperate to escape unhappiness. These spirits feel satisfaction at seeing a person fall even further and suffer even more misery. However, we cannot blame these spirits completely, because there is a part in all of us that derives satisfaction from seeing another's misfortune.

It is important, therefore, to establish a strong self that will not be affected by negative spiritual influences.

Worries and anxieties form unguarded areas in the mind, which allows spirits with a connection to certain religions to possess people. If many join a misguided religion, trying to escape their worries and anxieties, this religion becomes the dwelling place of large numbers of these spirits.

The spirit world is the world of thought, where those who have similar thoughts are attracted to each other, and those who have different thoughts are repelled. The Angels of Light and devils repel each other; in the eyes of devils, the Angels of Light appear evil, whereas to the angels, the devils appear evil. However, the truth is that good is on the side where God stands, and this can be proved through the connection to "happiness." Malign spirits are generally self-centered and search for happiness no matter what the cost to others. On the other hand, those God smiles on explore happiness from a perspective of how to improve the world so that the greatest number of people will be able to live in happiness. It is important to understand the difference between these two attitudes.

3. Lust

I would now like to talk about the spirits of lust. In the first section of this chapter, I explained that stray spirits are those who misused the freedom they were endowed with; the same is true of spirits of lust.

Human beings are free to think whatever thoughts they want, and since God divided people into male and female, it is only natural that men should look well upon women and women look well upon men. However, depending on how this feeling is controlled, it can lead to either good or evil.

The order between men and women is protected by the system of marriage. This is because God hopes men and women will join together to create a home where they can work to build a utopia, and that they will achieve happiness. However, if men and women act solely on their physical instincts, this creates negative outcomes.

Essentially, men and women have a mission to create a utopia within the home, which is the core of an ideal society. Sometimes however, people become blinded by desire for the opposite sex and act on this desire. This is not right because it goes against the idea that creating utopia in the home is one way of creating an ideal society.

Although it is difficult to generalize and some cases can be very complicated, the important point is whether a couple intends to develop a sexual relationship based on their love for each other, or without love. This difference is what divides humankind from the animals. The very reason that human beings are human is that they have an internal awareness of right and wrong.

God endowed human beings with a sense of shame and feelings of embarrassment and I would like you to stop and consider why this should be necessary. The reason is that shame acts as a brake mechanism to protect people from falling into depravity. Young people in particular tend to have a strong sense of shame; they will restrain themselves from wrong deeds when they think they would feel ashamed if their acts were discovered.

A sense of shame is one of the most basic emotions; it protects human beings from degradation. The fact that this feeling exists as a part of our soul reveals that we are required to respect a certain degree of order. The reason we are not free to explore our sexuality at will is actually on account of the fact that we have been endowed with feelings of shame and embarrassment as an attribute of our soul. God planned that we should feel these emotions.

If people become obsessed with sex, they lose sight of lofty ideals and aspirations to better themselves, and this gradually leads to degradation. From ancient times, there have been numerous taboos connected to sexual matters, because young people tend to become easily obsessed by sex.

As long as we are born as human beings in this world, it is impossible to deny a certain interest in the opposite sex. But at the same time, we must not forget that our souls contain the mechanism to control and adjust this. People who exercise their freedom in a direction that goes against the true nature of the soul will experience negative consequences and will suffer in hell as spirits of lust.

These spirits of lust attempt to satisfy their cravings by taking possession of people on Earth and leading them astray. This is common in the red-light district of cities. If people go drinking there, for example, they gradually lose their rational powers and abandon themselves to sensuality, despite the fact that they normally live in a rational way and are immune to spirits of lust. They begin to crave neon lights, and as they walk through a red-light district, in many cases they are tempted by spirits of lust and reduced to becoming just like them.

In fact, people who fall prey to the temptations of the flesh have distorted powers of reason. If their rational faculty were to remain firm, they would not get involved in this kind of trouble. This is a very important point. So, in dealing with problems of lust, keeping a firm hold on the powers of reason is one way of solving them.

4. Animalistic Tendencies

Some people may have come across the idea of animal spirits, for instance snake spirits and fox spirits. Animals too are creatures of God; within their bodies dwell spirits that aim to achieve their own spiritual growth, so it is only natural that there are animal spirits.

You may ask whether animals can also become lost in hell after death and the answer is yes, because they too experience the emotions of joy, anger, sorrow and pleasure, just like human beings. People may argue that animals do not have emotions or that they are incapable of thinking, but it is a fact that animals are able to think to some extent, and most are capable of experiencing these basic emotions.

Even small insects are able to experience basic emotions in a limited form. They want to do what gives pleasure and avoid pain. They know both joy and sadness, and if this is true of insects, then obviously the more evolved animals are capable of a wider range of emotions.

During their repeated reincarnations, animals such as cows, horses, pigs, dogs and cats have lived in close proximity to human beings and because of this they are able to understand what people think to some extent. Some of these animals are able to think in ways that closely resemble those of humans. However, because they inhabit animals' bodies and are trapped inside an animal form, they are unable to express their emotions adequately.

So animal spirits really do exist but the question is, do the spirits of foxes or snakes try to possess and delude humans as tales of the East have told from ancient times? I would be lying if I were to deny it. Foxes and snakes are spiritually very strong, and they possess great spiritual power. As they have existed for a long time on Earth, undergoing numerous reincarnations, these animals have accumulated various forms of spiritual power.

The souls of all animals have different tendencies. Take snakes, for example. Snakes like damp places, they slither over the ground and are generally despised by humans. The reason they are so despised may be that they look grotesque, and they also have a vicious, merciless nature. Snakes do actually have these tendencies; as a result of exercising the freedom of their souls, they have acquired these tendencies and manifest on Earth in the form of snakes.

Animal spirits that wander after death gather around people who have strong desires. Unlike humans, animals cannot understand anything difficult, but they do possess basic desires—hunger, wanting to be strong and to live a long time—so they are attracted to the human desires and by feeding off them, alleviate their pain.

Many lost animal spirits suffer great hunger, but as they are incapable of eating, they suffer even more. Eventually, their unattainable desires become uncontrollable, and they cause all kinds of harm to humans, for example, possessing people and causing them to suffer with rheumatism, aching shoulders or headaches.

As well as these spirits, there are other animal spirits that are not simply lost animal spirits. There is a part of hell that is known as the Hell of Beasts, or the Hell of Animals. Because the spirit world is a world of thought, the inhabitants take on a form that is an exact reflection of their thoughts. For instance, someone who is extremely brutal and vengeful will gradually take the form of a snake because their thoughts manifest in their external appearance. Someone who enjoys cheating others, thinking only of his own profit and acting in a very egotistical way, will be transformed into a fox. If these spirits have taken an animal form for several hundred years, they will begin to believe that they really are snakes or foxes. So there are spirits who believe themselves to be animal spirits but who are in fact humans. This is another kind of animal spirit that exists.

If a spirit has taken the form of an animal for too long, it will be tainted with an animal consciousness. Then there is the possibility it will be born as an animal in the next incarnation, though this happens to only a small minority of spirits. However, to be reborn as an animal is still a degradation for a human spirit. These types of spirits can be seen in dogs, for example, which seem to express almost human emotions or in other animals that are devoted to human beings.

However, this degradation is only temporary and in the long term, such spirits are actually evolving. By experiencing a life with animal attributes, they become able to see human dignity with a new perspective. This experience is similar to that of retired directors or presidents of companies who through reflection gain a different perspective on their past position. Although they may have believed that all their achievements were the result of their own abilities, after retiring they discover that they were only able to do their job with the help of the company. Bureaucrats have the same experience; those who used to swagger and thought they were something special when they worked for a government ministry discover after retirement that they were not as special as their position led them to believe.

What is the fundamental difference between real animal spirits and those human spirits who take an animal form? What it comes down to is that the latter were people who lost a sense of pride in their humanity, who did not attempt to use their freedom in a higher way to create something of worth, and did not take the opportunity they were given. In other words, it can be said that they are less developed spirits, pursuing a high degree of freedom on the path to human dignity.

5. Hatred

I would like to finish this chapter by talking about vengeful spirits. These are spirits filled with bitterness and spite. Some people believe that the way in which people meet their death is very important and this is most certainly true. Some also believe that people who die with hatred in their hearts will return as ghosts. It does happen that if people have died holding strong grudges, they are unable to let go of them even after death and, as a result, possess others or cause unhappiness.

This is not only true of the spirits of the dead; grudges held by the living also have the same effect. If a person holds strong feelings of hatred and resentment, these feelings will be transmitted to their object all day long. As a result of the vibration of these negative thoughts, the victim will begin to suffer a lot of pain, and sometimes become tired or fall ill. So if you constantly feel there is something wrong with you for no particular reason, or if many misfortunes occur in your life, you need to think about whether you are the object of hatred of someone, either dead or alive.

If you know of someone who died nursing a grudge against you, try to practice the following: First, study the Truth every day and live according to the teachings. Secondly, if you did something wrong to the person to make them hate you, sincerely repent your actions. Thirdly, try to convey the Truth that you have understood directly to them. You need to help the person realize how wrong it is to remain lost by embracing hatred. You can achieve this through "thinking." If you have truly understood, what you have learned will be transmitted to the dead person.

The resentment of the living is also very powerful and, in some respects, those who are alive can exert a stronger power than the spirits of the dead. Someone may hold a grudge, for example, "He stood in the way of my promotion," "I failed because she tricked me," "My marriage failed because he betrayed me," or "She stole the only person I ever wanted to marry." If you are the target of a lot of this kind of hatred, it is unlikely that you will be able to achieve success or happiness.

One way to free yourself of hatred and resentment is by self-reflection. If you believe yourself to be the target of a grudge, you should reflect on why you have incurred this ill-will and repent what you think you have done wrong. If such targeting is the result of your desires or egotism, you should apologize directly to the person in question or, if this is not possible, ask for forgiveness from that person in your heart.

In some cases, it may all be the result of a misunderstanding. If this is the case, try to explain the true situation. If this is impossible, reconcile yourself with that person in your own heart, or ask your guardian and guiding spirits to communicate with the other person's guardian spirit so that the relationship will be mended.

If you reflect on your past and realize that you are at fault, you should do whatever is necessary to solve the problem. Even if you are not responsible for the difficulty, do not blame the other person. Instead, if there is something about them that is praiseworthy, then by all means offer words of praise and try to see the person in a more positive way.

If you have attracted their resentment it is because you have only been looking at their negative traits. You must stop this. Instead, if you find one thing you dislike about them, at the same time discover one good point. If you find three things you do not like about them, think of at least three things you can appreciate. It is important that you adopt this way of thinking.

It is true that the mind of someone standing in your way is a mirror that reflects your own thoughts. If, within your own mind, you change the way you feel toward that person, you will find that he or she will change too. The reason for attracting the resentment of another must be that both the target and the holder of the resentment do not hold the other in high regard or ignored the other. If, after considering these two reasons, you feel that you shoulder some of the responsibility, it is very important that you apologize in good faith, or look for the other person's good points to praise or appreciate. This is the way to free yourself from the resentment or grudges of others, either dead or alive.

No one enjoys being hated by another and no one with this problem manages to get ahead in life, so do not attract others' resentment. To achieve this, you should live every day in a humble way, with gratitude. If you attract someone's hatred without ever having hurt them, it is because you either try to monopolize the love of others or you have a tendency to show off. You are ostentatious about something or you appear too proud to others. So if you find you tend to be the object of other people's resentment, it is because you have still not attained an appropriate degree of humility; you are lacking humility and a sense of gratitude. You need to think about how to live with a selfless heart.

I have described the various aspects of stray spirits. Each point I have described could very easily happen in the inner world of an individual. If you find any of these symptoms in your own mind, stop and enter into self-reflection. When you find what is wrong, apologize sincerely to God and vow that you will not make the same mistake again. The right attitude for those who live according to the Truth is always to correct any mistakes, aiming for further spiritual growth with a pure heart.

CHAPTER FIVE

Overcoming Negative Influences

1. Enrich Your Spiritual Understanding

In this chapter, I would like to explain how to confront negative spiritual influences and overcome the problems that arise from these. The cause of these sorts of problems is that people rarely have a precise understanding of spiritual matters; they are unaware of the true nature of stray spirits and so they do not know how to cope with them.

When you are physically ill, a doctor can provide you with a prescription for drugs or even perform an operation to cure you. However, when it comes to emotional and mental suffering, it is almost impossible to find anyone who can write you a prescription. So each individual must act as their own physician and write their own prescription. This gives rise to many different kinds of problems.

A person of religion is essentially a "doctor of the soul" who is supposed to be able to write prescriptions to cure maladies of the soul. Today, however, there are so many "pseudo-doctors" that it is difficult to get satisfactory treatment. For this reason, it is necessary to take a fresh look at true spiritual knowledge and, in doing so, promote the advancement of "medical studies" of the soul. In the field of medical science, there is a comprehensive system of theories to back up clinical treatment. Doctors are able to cure patients who have different illnesses because they have medical knowledge. In the field of spirituality, however, such basic theories are lacking.

Today, different religions compete with one another to attract more followers, each claiming to represent the only true faith, and the main concern of the general public is which religions to believe. Medical science can be roughly divided into Western and Eastern medicine, and in each field, doctors explore the effects of cures and remedies in an objective way. In the field of spirituality, however, there has been almost no research and there is no clear knowledge about what kind of "cures" or "treatments" are effective. The problem is that although there are subjective ways of assessing cures, there are no objective standards.

When fighting against spirits that have a negative influence, enriching spiritual knowledge is essential. First, it is necessary to know the true nature of these spirits. The existence of stray spirits should not be a matter of indifference; it is important to know that a stray spirit is a soul who is sick at heart and it is possible for anyone to become one. This means that if you die while suffering from sickness of the soul, there is a strong possibility of becoming a stray spirit once you return to the other world.

What does it mean to suffer from sickness of the soul? At the very least, it means that you are not filled with feelings of happiness but instead you are suffering and distressed. At times, people may feel very negative about themselves or become obsessed with negative feelings toward others. If people find themselves in such extreme states, they begin to create suffering, for example, not knowing how to be content, complaining, grumbling, becoming suspicious, frustrated, over-assertive, or suffering from an inferiority complex. Their behavior is like that of a fly trapped inside a small glass box and, not realizing it is caged, flying round and round, battering itself against the walls. This is the way human beings behave when they are caught in a whirlpool of worries. For this reason it is important to consider whether there is any possibility of your becoming a stray spirit. You need to know that it is possible you could be led astray.

The principle "like attracts like" is one of the laws that underlies this world and the next. There is always a good reason that stray spirits approach particular people; those people have certain elements within them that attract these spirits. By looking at the kind of spirit that is influencing you negatively, you will be able to understand what kind of mistakes you are making in your mind. In this sense, a stray spirit can be said to be your personal trainer. Those who are bothered by such spirits are not leading calm, peaceful, happy lives. Being under the influence of these spirits indicates that a person still has a long way to go on the path to enlightenment.

To enter the path to enlightenment, you should not rely on an outside power to expel such spirits; instead, it is essential that you look within, expel them yourself from within you, and remove the negative energy that is attracting them. Everyone has the seeds of evil in their minds that invite in evil from outside; this is expressed as "the evil within." After all, confronting spirits that have a negative influence does not mean fighting with spirits that are outside of you, rather it is a confrontation with the weakness in your own mind.

Stray spirits cannot come close to those who are bright and cheerful, who have no attachments and whose hearts are filled with light, because there is nowhere for them to lodge. You have to find out quickly how to restore a state of mind as clear as the blue sky. As long as you hesitate, your mind will never be clear.

A state of mind that invites stray spirits is just like a sky covered with rain clouds. Although the sun is always shining behind the clouds, it will not shine through them. Likewise, the clouds in your mind block the light of God, so the first thing you need to do is to clear away these clouds. To do this, you should carefully examine what kind of rain clouds might be within you. Then you will know what should be done to clear them away.

Worries are matters you think about all the time; in other words, they are thoughts that your mind constantly attaches to. Human beings cannot worry about two things at once. Although you may seem to have a number of worries, in most cases they all stem from a single cause. There is actually only one core worry. This, in fact, is the one that can cause the most damage in your life, so it is necessary to tackle the core of the problem head on.

What makes you suffer is a single thought or imagined idea. "That person is making my life a misery" is one thought, and it can be the cause of suffering. Comments made by others can also cause you to suffer. While one person thinks nothing of a particular comment, the same words may cause another person five or ten years of pain. What is the difference between these two people? I would like to explore this further in the next section.

2. Self-Confidence

Different people will react in different ways to the same situation. For example, if someone speaks ill of another, it will have a different effect from person to person. Some people will simply ignore a wounding remark and forget it altogether, whereas others will feel as if an arrow has gone deep into their hearts that cannot be removed and they will suffer endless pain. Also, there are people who accept criticism and reflect on themselves with humility, then try to correct their wrongdoing and ignore the rest. There are many different types of people, but one thing I can say is that the way in which you accept and reject external events or phenomena is a key to life.

I would like to emphasize here that one of the most important things that is needed to solve problems is self-confidence. Self-confidence does not mean overestimating
your abilities or being conceited. It is the indescribable
confidence that comes from the realization that you are
not entirely useless but have the seeds of potential. When
people are in the midst of pain or sorrow, they tend to
become negative about themselves and think endlessly
how worthless they are. However, it is important to see
yourself with a more objective eye, and tell yourself that
you are not as bad as you might think.

When you look back over your entire life, you will be
able to say, "I was wrong about this point" or "I should
have done better there," but at the same time you will
recognize that overall you did not do a bad job. There is a
realization that you were receiving love from God, and the
conviction that you have been of service to others. Self-
confidence is built on the accumulation of small realiza-
tions of this. It is important that you look at yourself in
various situations every day and, little by little, discover
the self who has been of service to others. Without a sense
of this, you cannot build true self-confidence.

Waterfowl floating on the surface of a pond have a
coating of oil on their feathers that repels water. Self-
confidence works in the same way. No matter what
misfortunes occur, self-confidence acts like this oil,
preventing damage to the depths of your heart. For
example, the amount of damage caused by the death of a

parent, a sibling, or someone close to you varies from person to person. Some people do not get over these things for up to ten years, others fall ill or their hair suddenly turns gray; yet others are able to carry on serenely with their lives. When a loved one passes away, it is important to be grateful for everything that person did for you while they were alive, and tell yourself that from now on you will stand on your own two feet.

In every situation, it is essential that in the depths of your heart you believe in God. If you believe that God created this world, then what may appear to be sad must have some purpose or meaning. It is unthinkable that God's intention is simply to cause you pain. You may become stronger through the death of a family member. You may meet an even more wonderful person through separating from a friend. You may find an even better match through breaking up with your partner. It is advisable to think in this way.

What is important is that with the passing of time you create a store of inner strength. Instead of struggling in pain and drowning in misery, you should work on refining your soul. At times like this, what is vital is to hold on to your faith in God and your love for Him. When you are caught up in a whirlpool of worry, ask yourself if you love God. Most people become obsessed with their love for themselves; all they can think of is how miserable they are, and they become desperate for the sympathy of others. But the problem is that no one ever gives them enough.

At such times, straighten your back and look up at the open sky. People who are in the midst of worry and on the receiving end of negative spiritual influences generally hunch close to the ground, turn their backs on the sun, and gaze only at their own shadows. As long as they do this, they will never be able to see the light.

So stand tall, turn your face to the sun, and stretch your body. This is an expression of your love for God. Do not always concentrate on the tiny being that is you but turn toward God and embrace feelings of gratitude. You need to realize the vastness of the love that you have been given, and remember that although you may be unhappy now, in the long term you will understand that what is happening is not really so very serious. In actual fact, the experience is providing you with nourishment for further progress.

No matter what trials await you, as long as you remember that you are learning lessons from each problem, you cannot help but become strong. If you have an indomitable spirit, things that seem difficult will never defeat you; rather, they will strengthen you. Those who are free and independent, and who have an indomitable spirit will never be defeated by hardships. To sum up, whatever the adversities you face, it is essential to see them as a hammer to temper and forge you.

3. Self-Reflection

Next, I would like to talk about self-reflection. We cannot talk of getting rid of negative spiritual influences without considering self-reflection. Self-reflection may seem a rather passive approach, but it is in fact an excellent method of confronting spiritual difficulties.

By observing the words and behavior of those who suffer negative spiritual influences, you will understand why it is an excellent method. What these people have in common is that they claim nothing is their fault. They complain, for example, that the system was defective, that the company they worked for was at fault, that someone hurt them, that they come from a bad family or were born in a bad area, that their family and relatives were to blame, or their physical appearance was the problem.

In complaining like this, they place the blame on factors outside themselves and this is characteristic of stray spirits. If you find this tendency within yourself, you should consider that you are either being spiritually influenced in a negative way or are a prime candidate for becoming a stray spirit in the future. You need to realize that when you try to attribute the cause of your misfortune to outside factors, you have become the target of negative spiritual influences.

In this case, it is essential to practice self-reflection. Self-reflection means looking back and examining yourself. When you feel like blaming others, it is important to look to yourself. But how should you do this?

First, you should ask yourself whether the cause of the discord lies not only with the other person but also with you. Check and see whether or not there were any problems that originated on your side. Then, if you discover that you have made a mistake, apologize to the person either directly or in your mind. Next, ask God for His forgiveness and resolve never to make the same mistake again.

A baby is born naked and knows nothing of this world, but as he grows up he accumulates many experiences and learns many lessons through trial and error. It is what he learns through this process that is most important. You should always have a positive attitude toward learning. Self-reflection is one way of learning. Human beings undergo many new experiences in the course of their lives and if you think you have made a mistake at some point, it is necessary for you to reflect on what you did.

The traditional Buddhist way of undertaking self-reflection is through the Noble Eightfold Path.[1] The first component of the Noble Eightfold Path is Right View, which means looking at things in the right way. This is checking to see whether you view others and yourself objectively, through the eyes of a third person. People are prone to see others and themselves from an arbitrary, biased perspective and think: "This person was born into a bad family, that is why he behaves in that way," "He is poor so he must have an inferiority complex," "Rich

1. Refer to *The Laws of the Sun* (Lantern Books, 2001), Chapter Two: The Truth Speaks, Chapter Three: The River of Love.

people are arrogant and exploit the poor," or "Famous people are all the same."

People tend to make these sorts of sweeping generalizations and simplistic judgments about others. They quickly make assumptions about how people should be— for example, "A religious person should be like this," or "A professional athlete should be like that." However, the truth is that people are all different, whatever the group they belong to, and it is almost impossible to understand a person's feelings after only a short acquaintance. Take, for example, people working in the same office. The working woman has her own worries, the new employee has his, and the middle manager, too; all have worries. Everyone has worries of one kind or another.

It is difficult to see others correctly. Even if you spend your whole life trying, you still may not be able to achieve it. You should never forget the possibility that although you see someone in a particular way, there may be a completely different way of seeing them. The same can be said of yourself. You probably have certain beliefs about what kind of person you are, but you should be open to the possibility that you may appear to be completely different if viewed from another perspective.

Next comes Right Speech. In overcoming spiritual difficulties, the practice of Right Speech is most important. When people are under negative spiritual influences, the first signs of these influences can be detected in their speech. Those who are always speaking ill of others and who are always complaining and grumbling are most likely being influenced negatively. If you find yourself speaking in a negative way, you should think about why you are doing this and make an effort to use more positive language. This effort will set you on a path to a happier life.

The Noble Eightfold Path also includes Right Effort, in other words, making an effort to follow the path to God in the right way. Spirits that exert a negative influence are only concerned with trying to corrupt people and are filled with a desire to make others suffer the same pain as they themselves endure. As a result, they do not like people who hold to aspirations and make an effort. However, these spirits can delude even those with aspirations, those who quickly become arrogant, over-assertive, or are ego-centered. On the other hand, they cannot affect those who are constantly moving forward and reflecting on themselves with humility; there is no way they can influence these people.

Someone qualified in a martial art like karate or judo will usually be polite and well-mannered. Those who are truly strong treat others gently. For example, someone who has a black belt in kendo (Japanese sword fighting) will not have any desire to hit another over the head with a stick, and someone with a black belt in judo will not want to throw a stranger he meets in the street.

Criminals or delinquents, on the other hand, will destroy things, and lash out at others. Those who use violence in this way lack the will to focus their energy through sports. In fact, they have no intention of making Right Effort. If these people really wanted to prove how strong they were, they should do it through a martial art such as judo, kendo or karate, but they never do. In contrast, those who have trained properly at a sport or martial art are gentle and considerate to others. Herein lies the difference between good spirits and others. If you make a genuine effort to follow the right path, you will improve yourself and you will eventually be free from any desire to hurt others.

Right Mindfulness, or having a rightful will, is also important in the Noble Eightfold Path. When practicing self-reflection, the aspect of the control of the will should not be neglected; you need to be aware of your will throughout the day. Your will reveals the kind of person you are and it is the will that distinguishes a saint from an ordinary person. The thoughts that occupy a saint's mind all day are different from the thoughts of an ordinary person, and the same is true of the thoughts of high spirits. They view things from a higher perspective, think about things from a broader, richer and more generous stand-point, and always wish to guide as many people as possible. On the other hand, ordinary people are interested only in themselves, and look at things from this perspective; their use of will is very different from that of a saint.

The same holds true for the way in which people approach others. There is a huge difference between those who approach others with the intention of guiding them and those who approach others with the intention to hurt. In fact, people who should be most admired in this world are those who are always thinking of the happiness of the greatest number of people. During the course of your life, how many people's happiness have you sincerely wished for, and then actually taken some action? This is the essence of being human. To this end, I would like you to examine your will at least once a day.

The Noble Eightfold Path also includes the path of Right Thought, which means to think in the right way. The "thought" of Right Thought refers to what comes into and what goes out of your mind. You need to observe the thoughts that enter your mind as you face the many different situations in a day, and control these thoughts. In contrast, the will behind Right Mindfulness is a sense of direction, what you intend to do in the future. So in practicing Right Mindfulness, you are required to make an effort to ensure that your will is not focused in a wrong direction, but continues to be directed toward God.

In this way, through practicing self-reflection, you will discover the balanced self in you, which is undistorted, well-shaped and highly refined. By becoming well-balanced, you will leave no room for stray spirits to delude you. Spirits that have a negative influence always try to attack a person at his or her weakest point; this is one of their characteristics. They will concentrate their energy on the darkness in a person or the part that is unbalanced, so it is important not to create this kind of weakness.

In this context, self-reflection can be said to be the most secure defense against negative spiritual influences. While being the best defense, it also works as the most powerful offense, because in the process of defending yourself, you give off thoughts that stray spirits hate. Just as mosquitoes hate to come close to mosquito-repelling incense, these spirits do not want to approach someone who practices self-reflection. A stray spirit is like a mosquito; if "mosquitoes" are flying round and trying to suck your blood, it is important to give off what they most dislike.

What stray spirits hate most is a right way of living. To restore a right way of living, you need to practice self-reflection. By doing this, you will be able to prevent these spirits from coming near to you.

4. The Philosophy of Positive Thinking

The next method of confronting spiritual difficulties that I would like to discuss is the philosophy of positive thinking. Those who are involved in spirituality will become spiritually sensitive and they may sometimes be on the receiving end of negative spiritual influences. It often happens that when stray spirits approach, a victim feels unwell and heavy in the head.

One of the most effective measures against this is positive thinking, which is the idea of dispelling darkness with light. It is very difficult to extinguish darkness, but by making an effort to increase the light, the darkness will naturally disappear. If you are in a pitch-black room, it is impossible to disperse the darkness, but once you turn on the light, the darkness will disappear. If it is still dark with one candle, light more candles. This is what positive thinking is.

If there were numerous muggings on a particular street at night, we would solve this problem by increasing the number of streetlights to make the area better lit. The same reasoning applies in dealing with the darkness in your mind; thieves rarely appear on brightly lit streets. If you think positively and live cheerfully, you will find that it has the effect of preventing negative situations from happening. This is a proven fact in real life.

Who do you feel better disposed toward, someone who is always smiling or someone with a sour expression? Have you ever thought a smiling face unattractive? No matter who the smile belongs to, it is attractive. A smile is something that has been given to us as a form of compassion. Is anyone displeased to see someone who is cheerful? It is likely that people who dislike cheerful people around them are under negative spiritual influences. Normally, people feel happy and refreshed to meet someone with a bright manner.

So one method of dispelling negative spiritual influences is to radiate a stronger light. Instead of trying to eliminate or fight against these influences, you can expel them by increasing your inner light, that is to say, by making your thoughts more positive and radiating the light of your inner self. Everyone has some darkness in their mind, "the evil within," which invites evil from outside, so first it is essential to eliminate this darkness with light.

The darkness consists mostly of negative emotions, such as worries and complaints. Worries about the future and complaints about the past are what attract negative spiritual influences. But is it really true that your past was filled with unhappiness? Certainly, you may have experienced a lot of suffering, but somehow you have probably managed to get over it. If you think back over your life and see nothing but a succession of failures, the way you see things lacks balance. It may be true that you have experienced failure, but it is very unlikely that your whole life has been a failure. So the problem does not lie in the facts, but rather in the way you judge them; you may have smeared your past with black crayon.

Positive thinking is one method of transforming a black assessment to a golden one. Even if you have experienced many kinds of pain and suffering in the past, it is the lessons you have learned and the value gained from these experiences that becomes the material to make your life radiant.

Through failure, human beings learn many things. Thomas Edison is said to have experienced hundreds of failures before finally succeeding in inventing the electric light bulb. However, for Edison who practiced positive thinking, they were not failures but rather the proofs that certain methods did not lead to success. This is how he interpreted his experience.

In the same way, instead of writing off failure simply as failure, it is important to tell yourself that you have learned which methods are not right and find another way. Then the next time you encounter a similar situation, you simply need to take a different path. Your past is not cursed nor does it bind you; rather it provides you with the material for self-improvement and presents a range of ways that should be avoided in the future to achieve happiness. Seen from this perspective, your past will appear marvelous.

As for the future, it is essential to have the self-confidence to believe that no matter what happens, you will somehow be able to get over it. Those who have a strong sense of unhappiness and believe that the future is going to punish them are overly concerned with themselves. Their over-concern with themselves makes them believe that if they imagine the worst that could ever happen to them, they will have no need to fear anything else. But this attitude only leads to unhappiness. Instead, it is important to think in a more positive way, telling yourself that yesterday things worked themselves out, and today they are working themselves out, so they are sure to do the same again tomorrow. Even if a crisis does occur tomorrow, wasting your time worrying about it today will not have any positive effect. It is important to believe in and make an effort to create a positive future.

Another important aspect of positive thinking is manifestation of will. The will of human beings manifests itself. If you have positive, constructive thoughts, you will find yourself in positive and constructive situations, but if your mind is filled with passive, negative thoughts, the same sort of passive and negative situations will unfold around you. In this respect, the techniques of self-actualization that are popular today are to be appreciated, because it is a fact that a bright future will open before those who are constantly planting positive, constructive thoughts in their minds.

I would like all of you to succeed in achieving self-realization in the right way. Discover your future self that shines brilliantly and use this image to achieve magnificent success. I believe that for a human being, supreme success means broadening and deepening one's character, having a positive influence on as many people as possible, and guiding others in the right direction. It is essential to walk this path with courage.

As long as your will is not positive and you are overwhelmed by dark, negative emotions, you will never find happiness. I would like you to value the philosophy of positive thinking as the basis for happiness, and value self-actualization as the method for achieving this.

5. Immersing Yourself in Work

I would like to finish this chapter on overcoming spiritual difficulties by talking about immersing yourself in work.

To sum up, those who have problems with negative spiritual influences create unguarded areas in their minds that allow stray spirits to sneak in. If people are caught up with worries and suffering, and live lives of frustration, these spirits are able to find a way in. So as not to leave any area within unguarded, it is necessary to immerse yourself in what is most important to you, in other words, pour the greatest part of your energy into what you think is of the greatest value.

If you are being negatively influenced spiritually, it is important not to spend too much time thinking about it. Concentrate on what you need to do in the present, the work you have at hand. It is no excuse to say that you are unhappy because you are the victim of negative spiritual influences. Similarly, being hurt by someone's comments is also not an excuse. Just as it is up to the person who speaks to determine what they want to say, so it is up to you to determine how you receive what has been said. You cannot blame others or your environment for your own hurt.

Instead of giving way to pessimistic thoughts or negative emotions, it is essential to concentrate on what you think is most important. If you are wasting time worrying, instead take a positive step, even if it is only a small one. Human beings cannot think of two things at once, so when you are preoccupied with worries, immerse yourself in some activity. For instance, you could find new ideas each day to improve the way you usually do things and make progress; with this attitude you will eventually be able to achieve great success. If you find your work becoming routine and commonplace, consider how to find better ways of doing it, how to create more time for yourself, or how to spend your time doing something more meaningful.

So if you are in the midst of worry or suffering, put all your energy into what you think is most important. By immersing yourself in activity and keeping busy, you will find a way to solve your problems. For instance, if someone is inconsiderate, and criticizes you harshly about something you have done at work, it is no use getting upset. You should take it as a stimulus to do better, tell yourself that there is always room for improvement and make up your mind to accumulate further good results. If you can think in this way, the more you are criticized, the better the results you will be able to achieve, and then the criticism will be something to be thankful for.

When others praise you at work, you feel happy and make more progress. Even in adverse situations where others are criticizing or bad-mouthing you, if you can understand that it means you need to be more humble and make more effort, the result will also be positive. God will certainly open up a path before the kind of person who always tries to move forward, no matter what happens. People in this world, too, will open up a path before you.

We are deeply moved when we see people making their way courageously forward with strong convictions, no matter how they are criticized or blamed. At times, you may be obsessed by different kinds of worries and anxieties, but these are the very occasions when you need to have a resolute attitude and hold on to your convictions.

I have just explained that immersing yourself in activity and leading a busy life is an effective method of fighting against negative spiritual influences and overcoming spiritual difficulties. I would like you always to remember this. If you are overwhelmed by worries, try to increase the amount of time you are active or take on some new activity. If you are not engaged in work, it is important not to restrict yourself to your usual routine, but to start studying something new and use your time in creative ways.

To conclude, by turning your mind to more productive and constructive directions, you will be able to overcome spiritual difficulties, while at the same time becoming a better person. Soon the time will come when you realize that what appeared to be negative spiritual influences actually played the role of teacher, helping you to refine your soul. It is my heartfelt wish that everyone develops a positive, constructive and cheerful outlook on life.

CHAPTER SIX

An Unshakable Mind

1. The Awareness That You Are a Child of God

In this last chapter, I would like to talk on the subject that I have used as the title of this book, an unshakable mind. In Buddhism, from ancient times, an unshakable mind has been considered extremely important because most suffering and delusion in life stem from mental agitation One of the main themes for Buddhist seekers has been finding ways to establish a mind that cannot be swayed.

Apart from Buddhist seekers, if you look at the people you meet in your daily life, you may notice that those with a stable mind have a deep inner peace and, at the same time, they possess strength and reliability. Their determination to overcome any difficulty and their strong convictions become the foundation for leadership. The essence of leadership is never being upset by minor difficulties and having the strength to overcome any problem. The source of this strength is an unshakable mind.

There are many people who claim to possess self-confidence but lose it the moment a difficulty occurs, for instance, if they are blamed for a petty mistake. These people need to develop a truly unshakable mind. To achieve this, it is vital to awaken to the fact that you are a child of God, because without this understanding, an unshakable mind is only superficial. Our minds will not waver when we recognize that in the very depths of our hearts we are connected to God. Without this awareness, our lives will toss unsteadily, like leaves floating on the surface of waves.

If you are convinced that you are a child of God, you become stable, like a boat that has dropped its anchor. The weight of the anchor hooked into the seabed keeps the boat stable, and prevents it from drifting. In life, the anchor corresponds to the awareness that you are a child of God, and the belief that you are connected to Him. If you hold to this belief, you will manage to get through every adversity in life.

However, if this belief wavers and you begin to accept the idea that you are at the mercy of destiny, like a leaf floating on the river of fate, you will be at a loss. This will only lead to pessimistic thoughts, for instance an attitude that circumstances and people will hurt you, or that a tragic future awaits. Whether you live an unhappy life led by these sort of fatalistic ideas or choose to lead a positive life depends on who you believe yourself to be.

Those who succeed in grasping the fact that they are children of God and understand the true nature of a child of God are remarkably resilient. People who have managed to find confidence in themselves in the midst of severe ordeals have strength. It is often said that to know one's limits is important because those who know the exact limits of their strength and ability are strong. For example, people who have experienced war and lived on the edge of life and death often have nerves of steel.

From ancient times, it has also been said that to achieve greatness, people need to have experienced some difficulty or suffering, such as a serious illness, a broken heart, a divorce or losing a job. The reason these kinds of hardships are considered a prerequisite for greatness is that suffering and difficulty show us rock bottom, the most difficult times in life.

Those who know the "ground" at the rock bottom of their heart become so strong that they have the ability to get back on their feet and overcome any difficulty. Every time you face a difficulty, it is important to discover your limitations, and how much you can endure. If you can see situations in this way, it is not so difficult to find some positive significance in distress or difficulty. Through these sorts of experiences, you will come to know how far you can exert your strength when you are really driven into a corner.

It is said that to assess someone, you need only see the person at the heights of triumph and in the depths of despair. Those who, at the moment of victory, expose their egos and become conceited, and those who wail and cry out in times of despair are ordinary. Those who can carry on with life as usual and have an unshakable mind in such extreme circumstances are extraordinary for this reason alone.

Take Thomas Edison, for example, the great inventor who after many experiments obtained patents for a number of different inventions. One day, a fire broke out and destroyed his laboratory. When he saw that his laboratory had been reduced to ashes, he simply said, "Good, now I can make a fresh start."

A similar incident happened involving Thomas Carlyle, the British historian and essayist. One day, Carlyle asked a friend to read a manuscript he had been working on. However, after the friend finished it, he left it on his desk and fell asleep. When he got up, he found that his maid had taken it for waste paper and had thrown it away. When Carlyle discovered what had happened, instead of being filled with regret or anxiety, he simply started to write the entire book again from the beginning. After its completion, this manuscript went on to become a famous history book, described as an immortal master-piece. I see great strength in his attitude.

Carlyle had a firm will and the strength to make a fresh start, no matter what difficulties he encountered. Even when his earlier attempt was lost just at the point of completion, he had the perseverance to start all over again.

This attitude is very important. Those who believe they can start afresh from nothing at any time have strength. In contrast, those who become afraid of losing their position and try to cling to it when they attain a certain level of status or fame are weak and easily defeated.

Let us be strong like Edison, who, when his laboratory burned to the ground, said it was a chance to make a fresh start. Let us have the strength of Carlyle, who after his manuscript was lost, rewrote it to create an immortal work. I am moved more by the attitudes of these great men than by their actual achievements.

Dale Carnegie, who is famous for his books, *How to Win Friends and Influence People* and *How to Stop Worrying and Start Living*, had a similar trait. When he was young, he wanted to be a novelist, but the manuscripts of the two novels he wrote were both rejected by publishers. Following this, he did not attempt to write any more novels but instead wrote many wonderful books about positive thinking and self-improvement. These books ended up having a remarkable influence on many people throughout the world.

Carnegie never regretted that he did not succeed in becoming a novelist. He said that he was glad to have chosen his path. When told that he would never become a novelist, he was shocked and felt as if he had come to the end of the road. However, he finally got over this rejection and went on to become a thinker and educator. In this way, he succeeded in carving a new path for himself.

Good fortune can be found everywhere. With the belief that you will always find a way to access your potential, there will be no suffering or difficulty, no matter what the circumstances. The deeper you awaken to the truth that you are a child of God, the more indomitable your spirit will become. You should value this spirit, the spirit that no matter what happens, you will get back on your feet again.

2. The Uncut Diamond

I have explained the importance of being aware that you are a child of God; this can also be explained in another way, using the illustration of an uncut diamond. There is a world of difference between those who see themselves as worthless pebbles, and those who see themselves as unpolished diamonds. If you believe that your true self is a diamond, the more you polish your own self, the more brilliantly you will shine, and the light you radiate will encourage you further.

However, people are prone to sink into self-pity and think of themselves as useless or worthless. Some people even live out their lives in such a way as to confirm their own image of themselves as losers. Each time they experience some misfortune such as a broken heart, failure in a job, or sickness, they think they are good for nothing, and spend their lives reconfirming this to themselves.

However, this attitude is not right. These people have lost sight of the uncut diamond within. No matter how hopeless a person may appear to be, it does not mean he or she is in any way inferior; it only means that the degree to which the inner self has been refined is different. You should always bear this fact in mind.

The more you refine your soul, the more brilliantly you will shine. According to their level of brightness, people think of themselves either as a gem or pebble. It is no surprise that those who think of themselves as useless are regarded in the same way by others. How you try to overcome the fact that you think of yourself as worthless is most important. Unless you succeed in overcoming this tendency, you will never be able to make a true leap in life.

How can people who tend to blame themselves discover the truth that they are not merely pebbles but rather unpolished diamonds? People who have a tendency to blame themselves can be divided into two types. One type are the people who always think negatively. Such people are attached to experiences of failure, as if to confirm their belief that they are no good at all. The other type are the people who are usually very positive and overconfident but when something crushes this confidence, they completely lose all sense of their own worth.

However, you should not see yourself in a completely negative way, nor adopt an all-or-nothing attitude. Do not forget that while you do have negative traits, you also have good points. Without a doubt, there is good within you.

Although one person may describe you in a negative way, it is a fact that someone else will praise you. There are very few people in this world who have never been praised. Someone who has been completely ignored by the world or who walks in the shadows must have some good points; you can find something to praise about them. If this is so, why is it so difficult to find the good points in yourself? Look carefully at yourself, through the eyes of an objective third person, and see if you can perceive your own wonderful, radiant nature.

If you have suffered a setback, you may feel you have lost everything; actually you have not lost anything. Rather, the situation may be showing you your strengths or it may be unveiling your false self, formed as a result of leading a false life and worrying too much about how you appear to others. If you can think this way, there is still hope. Even if you experience failure in this world, it does not negate your entire worth. Your good points still remain untouched. Unless you adopt this sort of objective way of seeing, you will never be able to discover the uncut diamond within.

On the other hand, some people go too far the other way and become overconfident; they think that they are simply marvelous and, as a result, develop a personality that repels others. They truly believe that they are wonderful, the best in the world, so they will not take advice from anyone else and consider anyone who does not hold them in high regard mistaken. This certainly causes problems.

This sort of person cannot live in heaven. Heaven is a place where those who are harmonious live. People who keep others away, or who consider someone they cannot get along with to be their enemy, can never live there. Rather than these attitudes, you should try and find a way in which you and others can live together. If you have no intention of changing or improving yourself, you cannot say you are refining the unpolished diamond within.

No one would go out in public wearing a diamond ring that was dirty, saying a diamond is a diamond whether or not it is covered in mud. I am sure the diamond would be cleaned and polished before it was worn. In the same way, it is important that you carefully polish the uncut diamond within. People often comment on others' clothes, making remarks like, "How can she come to the party in such clothes!" I wonder why people are so indifferent when it comes to the "clothing" of their mind. Would you appear in front of someone who has attained a high level of enlightenment with stains on the garments of your mind? These stains are quite obvious to an enlightened person.

What I am trying to say here is that you need to clean your mind, too. Although you may have a high-quality suit, if you do not wash it, it will become dirty. You send your clothes to the cleaners to have them dry-cleaned, so why do you neglect your mind, leaving it stained and unwashed? Just as you clean your clothes, so you need to purify your mind.

It is only because you wash your dishes every day that you can enjoy delicious meals. If you placed food on unwashed plates, it would not taste very good. You can buy any number of new plates but still you wash your dishes every day. So why do you leave your minds unwashed? Just as you wash the dishes every day, you need to clean your mind. You are mistaken if you think this is too much trouble. How can you meet others and express your opinions with a mind that is not clean? You need to continue to reflect on these points.

3. Awaking From Delusions

In this section, I would like to discuss how to dispel delusions. To begin with, let us consider what a delusion is. When you are deluded, your heart and mind are torn apart by conflicting emotions. When you feel trapped in a situation where things have become so entangled that you can no longer see logical connections, you could say you are in the grip of delusion. At such times, you need to discover how to cut your way through the difficulties and find a way out.

To find a way out, it is important to check and see if you are denying your own potential, that you are limiting yourself. Some of the premises you take for granted may be mistaken. Take a worry about work, for example. There are people who have specialized in a certain job for so long that they feel they could not make a living doing any other work, but they need to ask themselves why they believe this.

If this is the case for you, is it really true that you could not do any other job apart from the one you specialize in? I would like you to ask yourself why you lack the courage and confidence to leave your job, and why you cannot believe you could earn a living doing some other kind of work. Some men attribute the reason for not having the job they would like to their wives or children and say, "For your sake, I have been doing a job that doesn't really suit me year after year, and I will continue to do it until the day I retire. If it had not been for you, I would have been free to choose any job I wanted, but because of you I could not." In saying this, these men try to impose a sense of guilt on their wives and children. In actual fact, it is their own problem, but because these sorts of people do not have enough confidence in themselves, they cannot help but complain in this way.

People also worry about their health; today this worry is very prevalent. Many people are anxious that one day they will become ill or have an accident. The system of medical or health insurance is effective from the point of view of social welfare, but if it is based on the idea that human beings will definitely get sick, this is a serious error.

Basically, human beings can lead healthy lives without much illness. You need to realize that it is the idea that illness exists which creates illness. People tend to think,

"If I get sick, I can go to the hospital," or "If I take some medicine I will be safe." Although this sort of thinking may be all right for people in poor health, it is important to avoid becoming too dependent on medicines. By nature, human beings are healthy, and the human body is not supposed to get sick very easily. If you have a strong belief in health, your body will naturally be stronger. For example, if you trust your digestive organs, they will work well; if you do not trust them and always take digestive medicines, they will gradually become weaker.

When worries about health arise, you need to find the child of God within you. The human body is not supposed to get ill very easily. In a situation where there were no doctors and no medicines, most illnesses would heal naturally. Doctors know only too well that it is the power of the patient that cures an illness. Medication and medical treatments can only aid the process of healing. If the human body did not have the power to heal, surgical incisions would never heal; because the spontaneous power of healing exists, gaping wounds close.

Other common worries are worries about money or one's financial situation. People are often afraid that they will not earn enough in the future or that their income will not increase further. One of the reasons that this fear arises is a lack of confidence in their own abilities. In this world, there are many jobs where you can create wealth. The sort of job that produces wealth is one which caters for a large demand. Work that meets a demand produces wealth, but jobs that do not answer any demand do not produce fortunes.

In each era there is always some need; people are always searching for something. It is important to be sensitive and know what this "something" is. If you succeed in supplying what people want, it will bring wealth both to you and others. For example, if you publish a book that people want to read, it will certainly be a best-seller; not only will it enrich the minds of many but it will also make the writer wealthy. This principle applies to work, too. Work that you develop by considering the needs of people today will be successful. The same holds true of songs. A song that attracts people's attention will be a hit, but no matter how often you release new songs, if people do not like them, they will not be listened to.

What is important is to develop an ability, a sensor, to discover what is needed. If you are capable of this, you will find that the path to success will open. So if you worry about financial difficulties, always think about what people want at the present time, and what you can do to benefit others. By considering these points, it is possible to solve financial troubles.

So far, I have described worries about employment, illness and money that people in this age seem to suffer from. As well as these worries, there are the worries that arise from human relationships. These are unavoidable. People create suffering in different kinds of relationships, such as in the workplace or in the family. When a new person comes into your life, sometimes you are taken along the path of happiness and sometimes along the path of unhappiness. You need to think about how to solve the problems caused by personal relations. The closer a person is to you, the more sincerely you should make an effort to create a good relationship.

It is necessary to think constantly about ways to establish better relationships, rather than simply judging others from the perspective of your own likes and dislikes. Take, for example, a relationship between a wife and her mother-in-law. If each tried to find and praise the good points of the other, no problems would arise. Once a wife has discovered her mother-in-law's good points, she should admire them unhesitatingly, and the mother-in-law should do the same for her son's wife. If they do this, they will be able to build a relationship of love and respect for each other.

However, if each begins to worry that the other might hurt her, the opposite situation will unfold. For example, a mother-in-law might start complaining that her son has changed for the worse since he got married and that his wife is not right for him. The wife will then be very sensitive to these negative feelings and come to dislike her mother-in-law; she will want to stay away from her. If, on the other hand, the wife hears her mother-in-law say that her son has a good wife, she will feel happy and like her.

This example demonstrates that the mind of another is like a mirror reflecting back your own mind. In fact, the image you hold of others in the mirror of your mind is nothing other than you reflected back to yourself. If you can accept this idea, you will be able to free yourself from the bondage of human relationships. So to solve relationship problems, it is important that you resolve first to give to others, admire and praise them, and nurture their strong points. If you do this, you may sometimes receive goodwill in return.

Simply put, boundless goodwill is necessary to eliminate the problems that arise in human relationships. I will develop this subject further in the next section.

4. Overflowing Goodwill

It sometimes happens in a company that a subordinate betrays his superior despite the fact that he has always been treated well and praised. The superior becomes angry and thinks, "I did everything I could for him, so I don't deserve to be talked about like that," or "After all the encouragement I offered him, how dare he talk to me in that way?" This is a common occurrence. As a result of ingratitude, many people become angry over the fact that they have done everything they could for someone, but have received nothing in return.

The same is true in parent child relationships. Although parents believe they have done everything possible for their children, the children may not make any effort to show their gratitude once they have left home. This often results in parents feeling abandoned. In the

world of arts and crafts, too, this is often a common occurrence. An apprentice will leave the nest of his master after
an apprenticeship of several years to become his rival. In
companies, a president will spend years grooming
someone to be his successor with great care, then that
person will leave the company to start a new business as
his competitor. When this kind of thing happens, it is only
natural to feel you have been betrayed and taken advan-
tage of.

The reason these sorts of emotions arise is that the idea
of "give-and-take" has infiltrated your mind. People
unconsciously expect that if they give, they will be given
to in return, and that someone they praise will come to like
them. To avoid this kind of disappointment, you need to
continue projecting a loving heart. When you do someone
a favor, you should not expect anything in return. Just give
and forget the fact that you have given. Unhappiness in
life starts with the attitude of constantly remembering
what you have given others and forgetting what others
have given you. The thinking, "although I did so much for
him, he didn't do anything for me in return," is the starting
point of unhappiness.

People often think, "I did so much for him, I loved him
and took good care of him, but he has done nothing for me
in return. He is so unappreciative." However, these people
need to be aware that there is a kind of immaturity in the
idea "I did it for him." When you give to others, it is
important to give freely. It is particularly true for kindness

and consideration; you need to remind yourself that love for others is a gift that you give for nothing; it is a one-way transaction. If you happen to receive love in return, you should consider it an unexpected bonus.

Do not expect any reward. Just give sincerely, and instantly forget what you have given. On the other hand, try to remember what others have done for you and feel grateful to them. There are so many ungrateful people in the world and you should be aware that you are no exception. Even if you believe you carved out your own path by yourself, it is an undeniable fact that in the process you basked in the help of many people. You have simply forgotten the goodwill and the heartfelt love that you received from your parents, your teachers, your friends, your superiors and your colleagues. That is why you complain, "No one has done anything for me" or "After all I did for him, he turned round and betrayed me." It is a fact that those who always remember what they did for others tend to be quick to forget what has been done for them.

When you do something for others, it is important to do it without expecting any reward and to forget what you have done. At the same time, remember what others have done for you and continue to feel grateful to them for a long time. If everyone adopted this basic way of thinking, the world would be a better place.

The problem with the idea of give-and-take is that it lacks a sense of overflowing goodwill. If you complain that someone criticized you despite the fact that you praised him, or that you helped someone to get ahead only to be ignored afterwards, it means you do not have sufficient goodwill. You take it for granted that if you are good to someone, that person should treat you in the same way.

This shows that your sense of happiness is so small that it can be disturbed by the opinions of others. In other words, your goodwill or happiness is so limited that you only feel content if others give goodwill or happiness in return. However, if you are overflowing with goodwill and happiness, these feelings will be sufficient to wash all negativity away.

So give overflowing goodwill and limitless happiness. Like a fountain, pour out infinite energy from within. Look at nature. In the mountains, you can see numerous springs where water comes gushing out abundantly. Do these springs ever ask for money? There are oases in the desert— do they ask human beings for even one penny? They just provide water endlessly, quenching the thirst of travelers.

When you buy pork or beef, you have to pay for it, but what do the cows or pigs ever get back in return? What are they given for sacrificing their lives? Have you ever thought about this? What about the sun in the sky? Does it ever ask for some return from human beings, does it ask for even one penny? Electric power companies charge money for electricity, but the sun gives us heat and energy for free. It is probably impossible to expect people on Earth to be like the sun, but at least you need to be aware

that in nature there are many of these overflowing blessings. In these blessings is God's compassion.

You should learn to be unconcerned about the ingratitude of others. To do this, you need to be aware that you
also have the idea of give-and-take, and a petty, cowardly
heart that tries to confirm its happiness with the opinions
of others. It is important to be generous-hearted, enriching
people with overflowing goodwill that gushes out like a
spring.

If you feel hurt by the remarks of others and start
complaining that you have not been rewarded or that other
people are ungrateful, remember the words "overflowing
goodwill." You should ask yourself whether you have a
heart that simply gives. If you are feeling frustrated at not
receiving anything in return, you had better not give in the
first place. It would be better for you not to encourage
others, not to have any intention of making them happy,
but rather to be content just living inside your own shell.
Once you have decided that you want to live to make
others happy and help them improve themselves, you have
to be determined just to give. I would like you always to
remember that you should not expect anything in return.

5. An Unshakable Mind
I have discussed an unshakable mind from a number of
different angles. In the end, the main issue is how much
work we will be able to leave behind us when we leave
this world. "Work" does not necessarily mean business

achievements; your life itself is also work. Whether you are an adult or a child, a man or a woman, just living your life is in and of itself a great work. To carry out this great work to completion, you need to have an unshakable mind—a mind that is not swayed, no matter what happens.

An unshakable mind does not mean being narrow-minded or stubborn; it is a determination to complete your life's work no matter what difficulties you may encounter. The purer your determination, the more heavenly your life will be. By an unshakable mind, I do not mean stubbornness. I am not asking you to contribute to humanity with stubbornness. An unshakable mind must be based on a love for God. It is necessary that you feel love for God and believe that you are one with the creator of the universe.

You need to be aware that your nature is the same as the nature of the laws and energy that govern the universe; you are a fragment of the energy of this great universe. You also need to know that you who have this nature are undergoing spiritual refinement on Earth, with your own unique character.

You are one fragment of God and you just happen to have a particular name in this lifetime. So as one facet of God's character, you should try to express yourself. When you do this, it is important that you resolve to realize God's ideals on Earth, no matter what obstacles you meet. Those who wrote great works or were considered teachers of life were in some way different from the ordinary person. The difference was their unshakable minds.

An unshakable mind is the firm belief that you are a fragment of God, the strong determination to try to bring light into this world as a representative of God, and the pure intention of creating a better world. The firmer and vaster your unshakable mind, the higher the level you will be able to reach. An unshakable mind is, after all, an indispensable anchor and energy for carrying out God's sacred work, a work that reflects God's will on Earth. On stormy nights, it serves as an enormously heavy iron anchor and, on fine days, as a prop for the mast. This is the unshakable mind.

I would like every one of you to realize the ideals that spring from the depths of your heart straightforwardly and wholeheartedly, without being swayed by life's petty difficulties or trivial worries. That is why I have written this book. I hope you will read this over and over again carefully, savor it, and absorb it as nourishment for your soul.

POSTSCRIPT

I have already published numerous books of the Truth, among them are *The Laws of the Sun*, *The Golden Laws*, and *The Laws of Eternity*. The flame of enthusiasm that burns within me to spread this Truth grows ever stronger and brighter.

In this book, I have focused on the idea of the Unshakable Mind. I sincerely believe that this new approach to the Truth will provide practical guidelines that will help people to solve their problems.

It is my earnest wish that the powerful spirit that is present in the words of the last chapter, "An Unshakable Mind," will provide a wind that fills the readers' sails, propelling them across the ocean of suffering.

Ryuho Okawa
President
The Institute for Research in Human Happiness
June 1997

WHAT IS IRH?

The Institute for Research in Human Happiness (IRH), Kofuku-no-Kagaku in Japanese, is an organization of people who aim to refine their souls and deepen their wisdom. IRH spreads the light of Truth, with the aim of creating utopia, an ideal world on Earth.

The teachings of IRH are based on the spirit of Buddhism. The two main pillars are the attainment of spiritual wisdom and the practice of love that gives.

Members study Buddha's Truth (the Law) and practice self-reflection daily, based on the Truth they learn. In this way they develop a deeper understanding of life and build qualities of leadership for society, enabling them to contribute to the development of the world.

SELF-DEVELOPMENT PROGRAMS

Video lectures and meditation seminars are held at each branch office. By attending seminars, you will be able to:

- Know the purpose of life.
- Know the true meaning of love.
- Know the Laws of success.
- Learn to understand the workings of your soul.

- Learn the importance of meditation and methods.
- Learn how to maintain peace of mind.
- Learn how to overcome the challenges in life.
- Learn how to create a bright future, and more…

IRH MONTHLY MESSAGES

This features lectures by Ryuho Okawa. Each issue also includes a question and answer session on real life problems with Ryuho Okawa. Anyone is able to subscribe to the IRH Monthly Messages. Back issues are also available upon request.

MEDITATION RETREAT

Educational opportunities are provided for people who wish to seek the path of Truth. The Institute organizes meditation retreats for English speakers in Japan. You will be able to find keys to solve the problems in life and restore peace of mind.

For more information, please contact our branch offices or your local area contact.

THE INSTITUTE FOR RESEARCH
IN HUMAN HAPPINESS
Kofuku-no-Kagaku

Tokyo
1 2-38 Higashi Gotanda
Shinagawa-ku
Tokyo 141-0022
Japan
Tel: 81-3-5793-1729
Fax: 81-3-5793-1739
Email: tokyo@irh-intl.org
www.irhpress.co.jp

New York
2nd Fl. Oak Tree Center
2024 Center Avenue
Fort Lee, NJ 07024
U.S.A.
Tel: 1-201-461-7715
Fax: 1-201-461-7278
Email: ny@irh-intl.org

Los Angeles
Suite 104
3848 Carson Street
Torrance, CA 90503
U.S.A.
Tel: 1-310-543-9887
Fax: 1-310-543-9447
Email: la@irh-intl.org

San Francisco
1291 5th Ave
Belmont, CA 94002
U.S.A.
Tel / Fax: 1-650-802-9873
Email: sf@irh-intl.org

Hawaii
Suite 19
1259 South Beretania Street
Honolulu, HI 96814
U.S.A.
Tel: 1-808-591-9772
Fax: 1-808-591-9776
Email: hi@irh-intl.org

Toronto
484 Ravineview Way
Oakville, Ontario L6H 6S8
Canada
Tel: 1-905-257-3677
Fax: 1-905-257-2006
Email: toronto@irh-intl.org

London
65 Wentworth Avenue
Finchley, London N3 1YN
United Kingdom
Tel : 44-20-8346-4753
Fax: 44-20-8343-4933
Email: eu@irh-intl.org

Sao Paulo
(Ciencia da Felicidade do
Brasil)
Rua Gandavo
363 Vila Mariana
Sao Paulo, CEP 04023-001
Brazil
Tel: 55-11-5574-0054
Fax: 55-11-5574-8164
Email: sp@irh-intl.org

Seoul
178-6 Songbuk-Dong
Songbuk-ku, Seoul
Korea
Tel: 82-2-762-1384
Fax: 82-2-762-4438
Email: korea@irh-intl.org

Melbourne
P.O.Box 429 Elsternwick
VIC 3185
Australia
Tel / Fax: 61-3-9503-0170
Email: mel@irh-intl.org

OTHER E-MAIL CONTACTS

Florida
Email: florida@irh-intl.org

Albuquerque
Email: abq@irh-intl.org

Boston
Email: boston@irh-intl.org

Chicago
Email: chicago@irh-intl.org

About the Author

Ryuho Okawa, founder and spiritual leader of the Institute for Research in Human Happiness (IRH), has devoted his life to the exploration of the spirit world and ways to human happiness.

He was born in 1956 in Tokushima, Japan. After graduating from the University of Tokyo, he joined a major Tokyo based trading house and studied international finance at the Graduate Center of the City University of New York. In 1986, he renounced his business career and established IRH.

He has been designing IRH spiritual workshops for people from all walks of life, from teenagers to business executives. He is known for his wisdom, compassion and commitment to educating people to think and act in spiritual and religious ways.

The members of IRH follow the path he teaches, ministering to people who need help by spreading his teachings.

He is the author of many books and periodicals, including *The Laws of the Sun, The Golden Laws, The Laws of Eternity, The Essence of Buddha, The Starting Point of Happiness* and *Love, Nurture, and Forgive*. He has also produced successful feature length films (including animations) based on his works.

Want to know more?

Thank you for choosing this book. If you would like to receive further information about titles by Ryuho Okawa, please send the following information either by fax, post or e-mail to your nearest IRH Branch.

1. Title Purchased

_____

2. Please let us know your impression of this book.

_____

_____

3. Are you interested in receiving a catalog of Ryuho Okawa's books?

       Yes ❑   No ❑

4. Are you interested in receiving IRH Monthly?

       Yes ❑   No ❑

Name : Mr / Mrs / Ms / Miss : _____

Address : _____

_____

_____

Phone: _____

Email: _____

Thank you for your interest in Lantern Books.